Collecting Western Memorabilia

Collecting Western Memorabilia

Tim Lasiuta

FOREWORD BY GEORGE COAN

McFarland & Company, Inc., Publishers

Jefferson, North Carolina, and London

To my wife Karen, who lets me pretend...

LIBRARY OF CONGRESS CATALOGUING-IN-PUBLICATION DATA

Lasiuta, Tim.
    Collecting western memorabilia / Tim Lasiuta ; foreword by
George Coan.
        p.   cm.
    Includes bibliographical references and index.

    ISBN 0-7864-1660-2 (softcover : 50# alkaline paper)

    1. Western films—Collectibles.   2. Western television
programs—Collectibles.   3. Western comic books, strips, etc.—
Collectibles.   4. Cowboys—Collectibles.   I. Title.
PN1995.9.W4L34   2004
791.43'6278'075—dc22   2003025329

British Library cataloguing data are available

Cover images: Cowboy hat, holster, wooden nickle and Indian head
coin ©2004 Photospin; lasso ©2004 Photodisc Green; cowboy bust,
Buffalo Bill photograph, shotglass and holder courtesy
www.collectorsbuyandsell.com and www.collectorswantads.com;
badges courtesy Tatonka Cartridge Co.

Manufactured in the United States of America

McFarland & Company, Inc., Publishers
  Box 611, Jefferson, North Carolina 28640
    www.mcfarlandpub.com

Contents

Foreword
by George Coan

It was a magical time to be young: the 1930s, 1940s and 1950s. It was the time of the onscreen cowboys.

Anyone who went to the movies in those years certainly knew what a singing cowboy was, and what an action cowboy was, and the difference between them. Gene Autry, Roy Rogers, Tex Ritter and Rex Allen were singing cowboys. John Wayne, Wild Bill Elliott, Allan "Rocky" Lane and Don "Red" Barry were action cowboys. Singing cowboys were all about romance; action cowboys delivered excitement, and lots of it.

Sound had been introduced to motion picture audiences just prior to the 1930s and that meant that when the cowboys sang or fired a gunshot, you heard it. It was almost like being there on the real prairie.

Maybe you grew up during that period. Maybe you learned about it through television reruns, Western festivals and events. Either way this book will be a valuable guide to collecting the memorabilia of the era, as well as a trip back to a more innocent time.

My good friend Tim Lasiuta has asked me to write a foreword and I'm honored. He has brought together information that may help the reader to find long-lost collectibles from childhood or add to a collection more recently begun.

You'll learn about Western film festivals and similar activities. You'll learn about possible happy hunting grounds where you may find classic collectible items, such as toys, film, videotapes, photos, posters and just about anything your imagination can concoct.

I've been collecting Western films and memorabilia for over 40 years and still enjoy finding something I don't already have. I have articles of clothing worn by such luminaries as Johnny Mack Brown, Eddie Dean, Peggy Stewart, Lash LaRue, James Brown (Lt. Rip Masters on *Rin Tin Tin*), Johnny Bond, Sunset Carson and Jimmy Wakely. My autographed photos and posters would fill two file cabinets, and I own over 300 horse operas on 16mm film.

As owner of a modern theater, I have a special place to show those great celluloid treats, and my friends and I gather at the theater once a month and watch a double feature, a serial chapter and miscellaneous short subjects. We call our group the Saddle Pals, and our meeting place is the Old Cowboy Picture Show.

Ride along with Tim as he takes you on a hunt for items from those golden days of yesteryear, when thundering hoofbeats and the William Tell overture hinted that some mighty powerful, action-filled entertainment was heading your way. When you heard Roy and Dale singing "Happy Trails to You," you knew everything was going to be all right. Mount up now and enjoy the trip, and a hearty "Hi-yo, Silver" to you.

George Coan, Trail Boss
The Old Cowboy Picture Show

Introduction

In the beginning, there was a boy — and there were cowboys.

Saturday morning television brought Roy Rogers, Gene Autry, and the Lone Ranger. Saturday afternoons brought improvised cowboy-and-Indian shootouts with family and friends. Santa brought Johnny West and the stable full of equine companions.

Yes, the era of the cowboy was still alive when I was a child, but it was fading. *Bonanza* and *Gunsmoke*, still on air, were the only prime time westerns. John Wayne had slowed down his production and soon would stop. Roy Rogers, Gene Autry, Hoppy and Rex were now relegated to Saturday morning appearances. Even the Dell western comics series, which once sold millions, was now gone.

Then one day I discovered my father's cache of old comic books up in the attic. I was hooked. Soon I became a passionate collector, at one point amassing almost 5000 comics (I'm down to about 2000 now). Among those I collected were western books.

I don't know where I got the idea to get an autograph on a comic but I think it was from an ad for *From Out of the Past* by film historian and writer Dave Holland. I wrote to Mr. Holland and mailed him a Lone Ranger comic, which he would get autographed for me by Clayton Moore.

I distinctly remember receiving it back in the mail: Number 122, the Gold Town issue, signed by Clayton Moore. "To Tim, Clayton Moore aka The Lone Ranger." The Lone Ranger sent a package to me. I was thrilled. Wow!

That was it: I had to have more. Who next, Roy Rogers? I had read David Rothel's biography of Roy Rogers and loved it. At the end of the biography was the address of Arthur Rush, Roy's agent for more than 50 years. He served as a contact point for Roy until his death. I saved the address and sent Mr. Rush some of my Roy Rogers books for Roy to autograph. In a few weeks they were back in my hands, signed by Roy himself!

Around this time, I found an almost complete collection of Lone

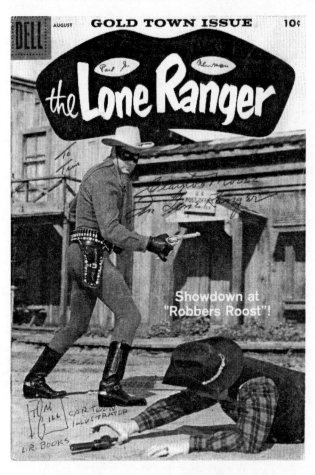

GOLD TOWN ISSUE 10¢

the Lone Ranger

Showdown at "Robbers Roost"!

Lone Ranger 122, autographed by Tom Gill, Paul S. Neuman, and Clayton Moore. (Author's collection)

Rangers for $5 each! I also started to find Gene Autry, Lone Ranger, and Roy Rogers hardcovers (Whitmans). Meanwhile, Gene Autry, Monte Hale, Rex Allen, Bob Hope, and others willingly signed books, comics and pictures. I was astonished.

All of this excitement was motivation enough to continue acquiring items, but then I discovered a new connection that made collecting even more fun. I learned my father had had lunch with Gene Autry, Pat Buttram, and maybe the Cass County Boys. He had won a coloring contest in Saskatoon, and the prize was lunch with Gene and his crew, and tickets to the show at the "Barn." He met Gene, had lunch, went to the show — and had no pictures! That's right, no pictures. How could you meet Gene Autry and not get pictures?

So I had to learn more about Gene. I read his biography, from which I learned that as good a cowboy as he was, he was more of a businessman. (Roy Rogers was more of a cowboy than a businessman, and he lived the cowboy life until his death in 1998.) I was hooked now on my own "business"— the business of collecting.

I have made contacts for collectibles through letters and advertisements that I found in magazines and collectible guides. I discovered the world of Lone Pine, California, through Dave Holland's excellent reference book on the Lone Ranger. I discovered the Roy Rogers museum through a biography of Roy and Dale. Through my membership in the Roy Rogers and Dale Evans Collectors Association, I found others with similar interests.

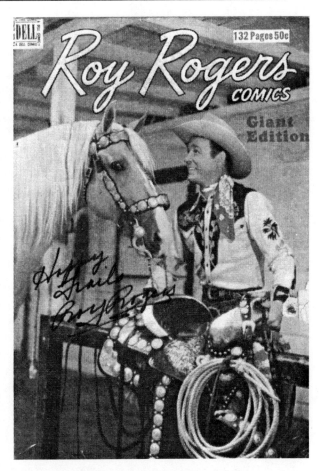

Once I logged on to the Internet with its almost limitless resources, my scope of collecting changed. I searched for every cowboy topic I could think of and soon found myself engrossed in the Old Cowboy Picture Show, Joe Konnyu's Cowboypal.com, the Old Corral, the Official Roy Rogers site, From Out of the Night, Steve Jensen's Lone Ranger tribute, and many others. From this beginning, I have

Roy Rogers Giant Edition, with autograph by Roy Rogers. (Author's collection)

spread out and worked on my own Web site, linking it to many that I was inspired by.

The greatest moment in my collecting life thus far was meeting Dale Evans at the Calgary Cowboy Festival on February 5, 1999. Though she was in a wheelchair by then, she still radiated energy. We met and spoke in a hallway, and she complimented me on my baby son — the last words she said as daughter Cheryl rolled her away were, "What a cute baby"! The next day, she spoke briefly to a standing-room-only crowd and then signed autographs. The crowd was rapt, even reverent. In my mind's eye, I can still see the scene. In my heart, I can still feel the atmosphere. I will never forget that day.

Dale Evans in Calgary. (Author's collection)

I believe that is one reason why I collect.

A copy of *Dale Evans and the River of Peril* is not great literature, but it is entertaining. It does not inspire me to heroic deeds, but it holds for me the memory of my meeting with Dale. For others, memories are triggered by an old comic book, a Johnny West doll, a cap gun, the sound of static over the RCA, or a 78 playing on the Victrola.

Therein lies the value of collecting: Memories.

I am not a cowboy. I do not own a horse. I have not ridden a horse in almost 15 years. I do not own cowboy boots, or a six gun. But I believe in the memories the cowboys have given me. I also believe in integrity of the lifestyle and image they represent.

We collectors know why we collect. We know what we collect. As collectors, we seek to preserve the "best of the west" and to integrate it into our lives where applicable. We seek to bring out the best of those who lived through the various eras and to pass it on in a way which contributes to the betterment of society.

We enjoy the process of finding and learning about the items we purchase, or would like to purchase. We like to make purchases, but often find greater enjoyment in the hunt than in the having.

This leads me to themes of this book.

Collecting.

Knowledge.

Memories.

Let us begin…

1

Heroes and Friends: Conventions and Other Gatherings

Our Western heroes have never left us. They may have passed on to the great corral in the sky, but they are part of our psyche. Their image may greet us at our daily computer screen, or their music may serenade us throughout our work day. At night we may relive their pulse-pounding adventures on our TV screens.

If you are fortunate enough to be near a metropolitan center, there may actually be a western fan club or, better yet, an occasional film festival near you. With the rise of the Internet and its vast resources and capacity for information, more people have discovered their "old heroes," and they are finding ways to get together in person to celebrate the ways of the west.

Need proof? Check out Roy Rogers.com and look under Roy or Dale's condolence page or fan messages. Look at Steve L'Argent's Lone Ranger page under the Clayton Moore Memorial. Check out the fan list page on almost any western themed Web site. You'll see: The cowboys are coming back to the corral.

From north, south, east, and west they come. Are you one of the approaching cowboys?

I am.

Let's put on our hats, boots and jeans, partners. Grab that precious Nudie sequined shirt and button it up. Pull out those Fanner pistols, and strap on a "Brown" gunbelt. The cowboys *are* coming.

We ride at first light.

In the convention halls across North America, "cowboy" gatherings are growing in popularity. Where once the major stars like Rex Allen, Roy Rogers, Pat Buttram, Russel Hayden, Pierce Lyden, Clayton Moore, Gail

Davis, Lash LaRue, Director William Witney, and other greats drove the convention trail, they have been replaced with lesser known but not lesser loved actors and actresses.

At today's conventions you can visit with many of the stars and costars of yesterday. A partial list of recent convention guests includes:

Jane Adams
Rex Allen Jr.
James Best
Peter Boone
Conrad Brooks
Harry Carey Jr.
Mason Dinehart III
Donna Douglas (Beverly
   Hillbillies)
James Drury
Beverly Garland
Gary Gray
John Hart

Will Hutchins (Sugarfoot)
Herb Jeffries (yes, he still attends)
Jimmy Lydon
Donna Martell
Jan Merlin
Mala Powers
Ted and Ruth Reinhart
   (entertainers)
Dusty Rogers
G. D. Spradlin
Peggy Stewart
Frankie Thomas (Tom Corbett)
Johnny Western

On the Convention Trail

The news is out: Someone in your area is actually hosting a western convention. You rub your eyes and pinch yourself. You're not dreaming! Hurriedly, you pull out your schedule book, flip to the correct month, and circle the day.

You are going.

"What am I going to wear? Hat? Of course. Boots? Better polish them. Pistols? Now where are they? Oh well, I could always find a new (old) set. Shirt? Sequin? No, too pretentious. Fancy? My Nudie? Done."

Of course, the day is almost three months in advance. But you have to prepare, right?

You pick up the phone, order tickets, and book the hotel. After all, you have to stay in the hotel, and if you are lucky, you will share an elevator with one of the guests.

Next on the list, toys. Autographs. Pictures?

"Do I have a picture of Harry Carey Jr.? Let's check. No, must order one. No let's make it six. Where is my stills catalogue?"

And on you go. You have known about the convention for only 20 minutes. And you have phoned your friends, booked the hotel, bought tickets, ordered pictures, checked out your wardrobe. Now you have to wait three months.

This is your first convention. What can you expect?

As William Sasser would say, conventions are an art form. An experienced organizer, Mr. Sasser has put together amazing conventions. He has sat on panels with Rex Allen — Jr. and Sr. — Harry Carey Jr., William Witney, Jan Merlin, John Hart and many others. He has met the "royalty" of his youth, and still retains his enthusiasm for the art form known as the Western Convention.

What is there to do at a western convention? Here are some possible activities:

Film viewings

Costume contests

Guest panels

Dinner with the guests

Chatting with the guests

Photo opportunities

The dealer room! (The best part)

Forming friendships

Reenactments (radio plays, shootouts)

Tours of movie sites (Lone Pine, Pioneertown)

Of course, the experience cannot be described. It has to be lived. The feeling of anticipation, the electrical atmosphere, and the sheer emotion of meeting someone who kept you on the straight and narrow cannot be conveyed with words.

I cannot describe the thrill that goes through your spine when you realize that you are holding the last issue you need to complete your Lone Ranger collection. Nor the feeling you experience as you discover a toy "missing" for many years from your storehouse of memories.

Enjoy it. Savor the moment. Breathe in the atmosphere. This is what makes memories.

A Short History of Western Conventions

Flashback to 1972: The Peabody Hotel, Memphis, Tennessee. Mitch Schaperkotter, Wayne Lackey, Tommy Floyd and Packy Smith organized the first official Western Film Festival. The first special guests were Sunset Carson, Lash LaRue, Max Terhune, and Don "Red" Berry.

The 1972 festival made a positive impression with the fans, so subsequent festivals were held again in Memphis in 1973 and 1974. The festival moved to Nashville, Tennessee, for 1975 and 1976. Festival organizers took a break in 1977.

In 1978, the Western Film Fair was held in St Louis. Promoted by Harry Thomas and Harold Smith, the fair attracted seasoned Hollywood and convention veterans such as Yakima Canutt, William Witney, Oliver Drake, Rand Brooks, and Kay Aldridge.

Meanwhile, back in Memphis, a dedicated group of fans began the show know as the Memphis Film Festival, which still runs today.

Milo Holt's Old Time Western Film Club took over the St. Louis show and relocated it to Charlotte, North Carolina. The Western Film Preservation Society was formed to organize and promote the annual show.

In 1980, the first Charlotte Western Film Fair was held. Harry Thomas managed the dealers' room, Bob Thompson scheduled the films, and Larry Reid supervised the banquet.

The Film Fair was very successful and ran in Charlotte until 1983, when a group from Raleigh headed by Ron Butler and Edgar Wyatt requested that the fair be held in their city. Charles Starrett was the star attraction and was named the honorary chairman of the Raleigh group.

Returning to Charlotte for three more years, the fair continued to feature the Best of the West. In 1989, Raleigh hosted the show again. In 1990 the fair moved permanently to Charlotte, where it remains to this day.

Around the country, western fans were gathering everywhere. The Buck Jones Festival has been running in New York since 1984. Ohio saw the Roy Rogers Festival (Portsmouth) and Hopalong Cassidy celebration in Cambridge. Tom Mix is honored in Pennsylvania.

Such diverse locations as Knoxville, Tennessee; Asheville, North Carolina; Lone Pine, California; Gene Autry, Oklahoma; Scottsdale, Arizona; and Williamsburg, Virginia, all feature festivals that celebrate the genre with style and grace.

Let's take to the trail.

Current Conventions

ASHEVILLE NC FILM FESTIVAL
ASHEVILLE NC

Held in of the original convention cities by one of the original film clubs, the Asheville Film Festival remains a bright spot. Organizer Tommy Hildreth and friends assemble an entertaining event early in November every year.

You can contact the festival organizers at:

Asheville Film Festival
Asheville NC
Tommy Hildreth 828-524-5251
cometvideo@msn.com
http://www.peedeeworld.net/cometvideo/filmfest.htm

Buck Jones Festival
Rochester NY

Dom Marafioti and Mario DeMarco and the Buck Jones Rangers of America celebrate the late Buck Jones every June in Rochester. Started in 1984, this event is one of the first and best.

Featuring the Buck Jones Silver Award, musical guests, and of course popular festival stars, the Film Festival never fails to entertain.

To get more information contact:

Buck Jones Festival
152 Maple St
W Boylston MA 01583
Dom Marafioti or Mario DeMarcos
585-359-8987

Calico Ghost Town Heritage Fest
Calico CA

Every Thanksgiving, Calico celebrates its heritage in grand style. Featuring ghost town tours, museum tours, musical performances, gunfight reenactments, shops, dinner and dance, and celebrity signings, the Heritage Fest is an experience you don't want to miss.

You can contact the festival at:

Calico Ghost Town Heritage Fest
PO Box 638
Yermo CA 92398
800-862-2542, ext. 0 or 760-254-2122
http://www.calicotown.com/heritage/

Charlotte Western Film Fair
Charlotte NC

Based in Charlotte, the Western Film Preservation Society has led the way with this festival, one of the oldest in North America. Since 1978, the society has presented western film screenings, held guest panels, and honored guests who have contributed to the genre.

Their impressive list of past guests is too large to note completely, but past attendees have been fortunate to meet stars long since passed on to Cowboy Heaven. A partial list of past guests includes:

Claude Akins   Bob Allen
Ray Aldridge   Rex Allen Jr.

Michael Ansara
Don Red Barry
Greg Barton
Dale Berry
Rand Brooks
Bob Brown
James Brown
Edgar Buchanan
Rod Cameron
Yakima Canutt
Sunset Carson
Michael Chapin
Frank Coghlan. Jr.
Tommy Cook
Ben Cooper
Alex Cord
John Crawford
Eddie Dean
Donna Douglas
Oliver Drake
Johnny Duncan
Don Durant
Jimmy Ellison
Gene Evans
Tommy Farrell
Kirby Grant
Alan Hale Jr.

Jennifer Holt
Lois January
Dick Jones
Victor Jory
Tommy Kirk
Lash LaRue
Alta Lee
Dirk London
Pierce Lyden
A. C. Lyles
Jock Mahoney
Jan Merlin
House Peters Jr.
Riders in the Sky
Dale Robertson
Joe Sawyer
Fred Scott
Gordon Scott
Linda Stirling
Gale Storm
Neil Summers
Hank Thompson
Johnny Western
Ray Whitley
William Witney
Sheb Wooley
Hank Worden

As you can see, the guest list is the Who's Who of western films. Tommy Hildreth, one of the founders (of more than one film society), must have one impressive collection of autographs and pictures.

The festival runs in late June and will no doubt continue to bring joy to many more western fans year after year. You can contact the organizers at:

Western Film Preservation Society, Inc.
4014 Churchill Road
Charlotte NC 28211
704-365-2368 Wayne Short
filmfair@aol.com
http://www.fortunecity.com/marina/coconut/2020/index.html

CHEYENNE COWBOY SYMPOSIUM
CHEYENNE WY

Cheyenne comes to life every Labor Day weekend with the sights, sounds, and smells of cowboy life. The Symposium celebrates cowboy culture with a full slate of activities that includes square dancing, storytelling, western poets, singers, histories, rodeo action, black powder and repeating rifle demonstrations, and much, much more. Special guests are featured yearly and add much flavor to the festivities.

For more information on the Cheyenne weekend, contact:

Cheyenne Cowboy Symposium
321 Warren Ave
Cheyenne WY 82001
307-635-5788
http://www.cheyennecowboysymposium.com/

COWBOY HERITAGE FESTIVAL
DODGE CITY KS

Dodge City's contribution to modern cowboy celebrations, the Cowboy Heritage Festival, is held late in May and combines the rodeo experience with the culture of the west.

Events include cowboy poets, storytelling, gunfight reenactments, parades, concerts, an 1880s cowboy ball, Wyatt Earp lookalike contests, authentic food and living history. In 2002, the festival included the Kansas Cowboy Hall of Fame inaugural induction. The Boot Hill Museum also opens up its secrets for all "myth seekers" to explore.

You can contact the Heritage Festival at:

Cowboy Heritage Festival
400 W Wyatt Earp Blvd.
Dodge City KS 67801
800-653-9378 or 620-225-8186
www.cowboyheritagefestival.com

END OF THE TRAIL FESTIVAL
CORONA CA

Every year, early in April, the End of the Trail Festival celebrates the best shooters in the "west." Home to the Annual Mounted Shooting and Skeet Shooting Championship, this competition draws the best. Past champions have included celebrities such as Rob Word, Ben Cooper, and Bruce Boxleitner. Other attractions include cookouts, vendors' booths, roping, musical entertainment, fancy shooting displays, scene reenactments, a Wild West Show, and celebrities.

For more information on this world class event, contact Mike Reahauges Shooting Enterprise at:

> End of the Trail Festival
> 5800 Bluff St
> Norco CA 92860
> 909-735-7981
> http://www.sassnet.com/eotdocs/EOTTOC.html

FESTIVAL OF THE WEST
SCOTTSDALE AZ

One of the premier festivals, the Festival of the West has seen excellent guests and presentations by musicians and cowpokes. Held since 1991, the festival has been named as one of the top 100 Events in North America and has even received the American Cowboy Culture Award (2000). The festival features mounted shooting competitions, chuck wagon cooking, cowboy poetry, Old West demonstrations, an art and craft exhibition, western costume contests, and celebrity panels and concerts. In 2002, the restored *Under Western Stars* (1938) and *Trigger Jr.* (1950) opened the celebrations.

An annual presentation of the Festival of the West is the Cowboy Spirit Award, presented to heroes with integrity, strength of spirit and moral character. Past honorees include Patsy Montana, Dale Evans, Roy Rogers, Gene Autry, Rex Allen, Ben Johnson, Harry Carey Jr., Denver Pyle, Jane Russell, and Bruce Boxleitner.

Held in early March, this show has always entertained fans of all ages and interests. You can contact festival organizers Mary Brown, Celeste Winters, or Wendie Marlais at:

> US West Festival of the West
> PO Box 12966
> Scottsdale AZ 85267-2966
> 602-996-4387
> maryb@festivalofthewest.com
> http://www.festivalofthewest.com or www.calliopeinc.net

GENE AUTRY OKLAHOMA MUSEUM FILM AND MUSIC FESTIVAL
GENE AUTRY OK

What better place to celebrate singing cowboys than Gene Autry, Oklahoma? Every September, the Gene Autry Oklahoma Museum hosts a three-day festival featuring the best of the singing cowboys.

Recent guests have included Rex Allen Jr., Roy Rogers Jr., cowboy poet Don Edwards, Dale Robertson, Mickey Dawes, Johnny Western, Les Gilliam, the Rockin' M Wranglers, Dick Vance, Cherokee, the Sons of the Pioneers, the Riders in the Sky and many others.

As an added attraction, the Gene Autry Oklahoma Museum is open for tours. As a tribute to the "B" western heroes, the museum delivers.

For those of you inclined to the music of the west, this is the place to be. You can contact the museum and festival at :

> Gene Autry Oklahoma Museum and Film Festival
> Director: Elwin Sweeten
> PO Box 67
> Gene Autry OK 73436
> 580-294-3047
> esweeten@brightok.net
> http://www.cow-boy.com/festival.htm

GOLDEN BOOT AWARDS
LOS ANGELES CA

Not really a convention or festival per se, the Golden Boot Awards ceremony is the best opportunity to meet and honor the Best of the West. Held in early August and organized by the Motion Picture and Television Fund and Rob Word (of Word TV), the "Boot" is the most prestigious award any cowboy can be given.

Past "Boot" honorees include Pat Buttram, Rex Allen, Roy Rogers, Gene Autry, Clayton Moore, Jay Silverheels, Chuck Norris, Tom Selleck, Dale Evans, and Monte Hale. Pat Buttram organized the first Golden Boot Award ceremony in 1980 to commemorate his comrades in film.

All of Hollywood goes cowboy to celebrate this roundup of stars. A benefit auction is held with proceeds going to the MPTV Fund. There is a mixer on Friday, and of course, the awards go on Saturday.

For further information on the "Boot," contact:

> Golden Boot Awards
> 22212 Ventura Blvd, Ste 300
> Woodland Hills CA 91364-1530
> 818-876-1900
> www.mptvfund.org

The Golden Boot Awards is the only major awards ceremony where fans can mingle with the stars. If you are able to attend, saddle up your horse and go! This is a once-in-a-lifetime event.

Hopalong Cassidy Festival
Cambridge OH

Hoppy, we saved up our dimes to come to your festival in early May. Yes, Hopalong Cassidy is celebrated in Cambridge, Ohio, and the cowpokes come from miles around.

Grace Bradley Boyd, Hopalong's widow, helps commemorate the memory of her late husband. Scheduled events include a western collectors show and sale, cowboy lookalikes contest, dinner with the stars, free Hoppy films, a Hopalong parade, and a street dance. As an added attraction, you can tour the Hoppy Museum.

You can contact them at:

> Hopalong Cassidy Festival
> 6310 Friendship Dr.
> New Concord OH 43763-4850
> 336-674-3431 or 800-933-5480
> Email: Lbates1205@cs.com
> http://www.visitguernseycounty.com/special.html
> (click on Calendar of Events)

Lincoln County Cowboy Symposium
Ruidoso Downs NM

Early in October, western fans can celebrate true western culture in the foothills of the Sacramento Mountains. Storytellers, musicians, chuckwagon chefs, cowboy poets, western artists, and vendors all gather together to "go country." Celebrated in association with the "Hubbard Museum of the American West," this event brings you deep into Billy the Kid country.

For more information on this event, please contact the festival at:

> Lincoln County Cowboy Symposium
> PO Box 240
> Ruidso Downs NM 88346
> 505-378-4142
> moth@zianet.com
> http://www.zianet.com/museum/LCCS.html

Lone Pine Film Festival
Lone Pine CA

What can we say about the best? Starting in 1989, film historian and writer Dave Holland, along with a committee of film buffs, organized the Lone Pine Film Festival.

Lone Pine itself is part of movie history. Its area has starred in westerns since the early 1920s when William S. Hart and his company filmed many silent movies there. The hills of Lone Pine have been seen in *High Sierra, Bar 20, How the West Was Won, The Charge of the Light Brigade,* and many Roy Rogers and Gene Autry films.

Dave Holland has written a book about Lone Pine and its Hollywood connection and leads a tour to the prominent movie locations in the surrounding area. Dave will lead you to where the *Bad Day at Black Rock* tracks were, where Tyrone Power walked the streets of "Salt Lake City" in *Brigham Young,* where the Lone Ranger ambush was filmed, and many more memorable locations. Definitely worth the extra $35 for the tour when you go to Lone Pine.

Held in October of each year, the festival does an excellent job of preserving and celebrating movie history. The goal of the festival is to build and support a film history museum that will pay tribute to the extensive history of the area.

Guests over the years have included Roy Rogers, Dale Evans, Gene Autry, Gregory Peck, Adrian Booth, Ben Burt, Loren James, Burt Kennedy, Roddy McDowall, Claire Trevor, Peggy Stewart, Clayton Moore, Ruth Terry, William Witney, William Wellman Jr., Dave Holland, and Ernest Borgnine.

Being a movie location festival, Lone Pine is unique. In addition to guest panels, film screenings, dealer rooms, and photo opportunities, it offers travel to the actual locations of classic movies. For the western film buff, this can be quite a moving experience.

Lone Ranger fans loved it when Dave Holland and the committee organized in the late 1990s a reenactment of the Lone Ranger ambush scene, complete with full orchestra and actors. No other place could do that.

You can contact the Lone Pine Film Festival at:

> Lone Pine Film Festival
> PO Box 111
> Lone Pine CA 93545
> www.lonepinefestival.org

THE MEMPHIS FILM FEST
MEMPHIS TN

Another talented convention organizer is Ray Nielsen of the Memphis film community. Thanks to Ray and an able group of capable cowpokes, the Memphis Film Preservation Society has presented movie festivals since 1971!

More than 250 guests have graced the convention floors of the Memphis show. The first convention featured Don "Red" Berry, Sunset Carson, Lash LaRue, Russell Hayden, and the recently departed Max Terhune. Subsequent shows have included many greats long since gone.

For each festival, multiple viewing rooms are available with up to 125 movies to choose from! A daily panel of stars, a great dealer room, and the chance to chat with both stars and fans always part of the action.

The festival takes place in early June, and every year, Ray and his committee have assembled an excellent lineup of guests. Past attendees have included Michael Chapin (*Rough Rider* TV series), Tommy Cook (Little Beaver), Gary Gray, Russell Wade, Bill Catching, and Miriam Seegar.

For more information, you can contact the organizers at:

Memphis Film Festival
PO Box 40272
Memphis TN 38174-0272
rnielsen@alltel.net
www.memphisfilmfestival.com/

THE OLD COWBOY PICTURE SHOW
LAURINBURG NC

George Coan and Leo Pando, co-trail bosses of the Old Cowboy Picture Show, have been entertaining cowboy fans in North and South Carolina for many years.

Not really a convention, but more of a Saturday matinee, TOCPS now takes place at the Cinema Twin Theatre in Laurinburg, N.C., showing a good selection of classic films and movie serial chapters on the first Saturday of every month. Admission is free, but donations are accepted to cover expenses.

Frequently attended by the Saddle Pal lookalikes, this event really keeps the spirit of the old west alive.

George and Leo also publish an outstanding newsletter.

You can contact George:

George Coan
PO Box 66
Camden SC 29020
803-432-9643 (res)
cowboy@aaahawk.com
www.cowboyshow.com

PIONEERTOWN
PIONEERTOWN CA

Founded in 1946 by Roy Rogers, Dick Curtis, Bud Abbott, Russell Hayden, Louella Parsons, and Phillip Krasne, Pioneertown was built to provide a permanent movie set for Gene Autry, the Cisco Kid, Annie Oakley, Judge Roy Bean, Buffalo Bill Jr. and many others. The facility is open to visitors April through November. The western street has been restored to its "original" condition and is home to reenacted gunfights as well as to Pioneertown Days. Associated facilities include the Pioneertown Motel, Pioneer Bowl, Pappy and Harriet's, Stud Valley Ranch and Diamond Locations (film services).

Pioneertown
PO Box 421
Pioneertown CA 92268
760-228-0494
http://www.desertgold.com/ptown/hayden.html

Yucca Valley Historical Society
PO Box 2046
Yucca Valley CA 91186
Over 140 Historical sites are represented

RED STEAGALL COWBOY GATHERING AND
WESTERN SWING FESTIVAL
FORT WORTH TX

Balladeer Red Steagall serves as the host of the Fort Worth Cowboy Gathering and Western Swing Festival held annually in late October. Held for several years now, this festival brings the best to Texas for a true family event.

Including a rodeo, cowboy and western swing music, young cowpoke activities, cowboy poetry, authentic chuck wagon competitions, horsemanship clinics, and a trading post, this festival brings together an outstanding array of talent.

You can contact the organizers at:

Red Steagall Cowboy Gathering and Western Swing Festival
PO Box 136639
Forth Worth TX 76136
888-COWTOWN
debbie@redsteagall.com
www.theredsteagallcowboygathering.com

Rex Allen Days
Willcox AZ

Willcox, Arizona, has paid tribute to its native son for 51 years now, making Rex Allen Days officially the longest running themed festival and western celebration. Willcox puts on a great show.

The festival is held in late September and early October. The Willcox Chamber of Commerce presents a movie festival (run in the restored movie house) and a rodeo (of course). Rex Allen Jr. makes the rounds with the reigning rodeo queen.

The festival also offers the opportunity to tour the Rex Allen Museum, home to the largest collection of Rex Allen memorabilia. Mary Leighton and her staff have done a great job of maintaining the Allen legacy in Willcox. The spirit of the favorite son, Rex Allen, the last of the singing cowboys, continues to watch over his home.

You can contact the festival organizers at:

> Rex Allen Days
> PO Box 207
> Willcox AZ 85643
> 877-234-4111
> ostark@vtc.net
> http://www.pinkbanana.com/rex

Roy Rogers and Dale Evans Western Film Festival
Victorville CA

The highest profile western convention is the Roy Rogers and Dale Evans Western Film Festival, which has been held since 1997 in Victorville, California. Usually held in late February, this show celebrates the legendary singing cowboy stars and features the Rogers family's best — all for the benefit of the Happy Trails Children's Foundation in Apple Valley, California. This festival has shown film clips from Roy and Dale's life and the very rare *Dale Evans Show* premiere which never aired! Dusty Rogers and his band, The Highriders, as well as the Rogers Legacy perform annually at this well-attended gathering in Roy's old backyard.

For more information contact:

> The Happy Trails Children's Foundation
> 10755 Apple Valley Rd
> Apple Valley CA 92308
> 760-240-3330
> www.happytrails.org

ROY ROGERS MEMORIAL FESTIVAL
PORTSMOUTH OH

The birthplace of Roy Rogers has commemorated its favorite son for 10 years now. Roy and Dale attended the festival in the mid 1990s; following their deaths, others have gathered to remember them. Usually taking place in late May and early June, this festival — under the capable hand of organizer Larue Horsley — has done an excellent job of remembering Roy and Dale.

A unique feature of this festival is the Roy Rogers tour. As Roy grew up in this area, it is full of Roy Rogers history.

You can contact the festival at:

> Larue Horsley
> Roy Rogers Memorial Festival
> PO Box 1166
> Portsmouth OH 45662
> 740-353-0900
> http://www.visithistory.com/events.htm

SANTA CLARITA COWBOY POETRY AND MUSIC FESTIVAL
SANTA CLARITA CA

Since 1997, Melody Ranch has been the home of the Santa Clarita Cowboy Poetry and Music Festival. Utilizing William S. Hart's nearby mansion and museum, the festival is held in late March or early April.

Featured events include musical performances in William S. Hart's living room, a trail ride, cowboy breakfast, a dinner train, western swing dance, live drama and poetry presentations. Entertainers from around the world all meet at Santa Clarita!

Melody Ranch, once owned by Gene Autry, is open to the public this weekend only. The festival affords the film fan a rare opportunity to walk through western cinematic history where over 750 westerns were filmed in the Golden Age of the Mighty B's. The William S. Hart Museum is also available for tours.

You can get more information on the festival from:

> Santa Clarita Cowboy Poetry And Music Festival
> 2920 Valencia Blvd., Ste 120
> Santa Clarita CA 91335
> 661-286-4021 or 800-305-0755
> http://www.santa-clarita.com/cp/2003/index.asp

SEDONA WESTERN FILM FESTIVAL
SEDONA AZ

The Sedona Western Film Festival is a great place to be. Held in May each year, it features the Silver Spur Award for outstanding contributions to the industry, a golf tournament, celebrities, gunfight recreations, western art, a frontier BBQ, and a mounted shooting competition. Another great feature of this event is the scenery you can "see" in your favorite movies.

The organizers can be contacted at:

Sedona Western Film Festival
PO Box 20549
Sedona AZ 86341
928-248-9697
http://www.sedonamoviestudio.com/festival.htm

TOM MIX FESTIVAL
DUBOIS PA

The first "King of the Cowboys" is celebrated in DuBois, Pennsylvania, in mid–September every year. The year 2004 marks the 25th anniversary of this festival honoring Tom Mix, a Pennsylvania native. Films, dealers, and special events are all part of this long-running festival.

You can contact the organizer, Georgia Slagle, at:

Tom Mix Festival
PO Box 402
DuBois PA 15801
814-371-5344
Georgia@key-net.net
www.tommixfestival.com

WESTERN LEGENDS ROUNDUP
KANAB UT

Home of the "Greatest Earth on Show," Kanab has celebrated the cinematic west since 1998. The town was the preferred western location for many stars; Tom Mix made *Deadwood Gulch* here in the 1930s.

The festival includes cowboy poetry and music, arts and crafts, street vendors, wild horse parade, a wagon train, Indian and square dancing, stage shows, a lookalike contest, great food, and much, much more.

Western history surrounds you here, so don't miss the Walk of Fame. Held in late August, this roundup will revive your love of authentic western culture.

For more information, contact:

Western Legends Roundup
C/o Kane Country Travel Council
89 South 100 East
Kanab UT 84741
800-733-5263
kane@westernlegendsroundup.com
http://www.westernlegendsroundup.com/

WILL ROGERS DAYS
CLAREMONT OK

A great tribute to the late Will Rogers, Will Rogers Days are held in early November for four days each year. The Will Rogers Memorial Museum is also open for visits during this time. Encompassing a rodeo, a cable TV tribute, a Rotary Club gala, a parade, a Pony Express reenactment, and a wreath-laying ceremony, the Will Rogers Festival is a great place to be.

For further information contact the organizers at:

Will Rogers Days
PO Box 157
Claremore OK 74018-0157
800-324-9455
http:// www.willrogers.com

WILLIAMSBURG FILM FESTIVAL
WILLIAMSBURG VA

One of the best conventions for many years, the Williamsburg Film Festival has consistently featured the best of the stars. Proposed guests for upcoming years include Jan Merlin, Jimmy Lydon, Jane Adams, Ben Cooper, Frankie Thomas, Ted and Ruth Reinhart, and musical performers.

Running in late February and early March, this show has featured a Tom Corbett radio play reenactment *Marooned with Death*, book swaps and sales and panel discussions.

With Bill Sasser and his gang at the helm of this festival, the future looks good for cowboy fans in the Virginia area.

You can contact the organizers at:

Williamsburg Film Festival
PO Box 524
Gloucester Point VA 23062

Ray Smith: 919-957-0222
Bill Sasser at wsasser@earthlink.net
http://go.to/williamsburgfilmfestival

The above listing is of course, not complete. The number of events held yearly is increasing again thanks to the rediscovery of Baby Boomer childhood idols, the rekindling of interest in heroes since September 11, 2001, and the efforts of the Western Channel and other stations to bring the cowboy back to North America.

2

Trail Whisperings: Newsletters and Magazines

The next best source of information to conventions is of course newsletters and magazines. The western themed newsletters and magazines available are well done and labors of love.

A list of present newsletters and magazines follows:

American Cowboy
PO Box 6630
Sheridan WY 82801
www.americancowboy.com
(The best selling western magazine today)

The Big Trail
540 Stanton Ave
Akron OH 44301
(Great for John Wayne fans)

Buck Jones Western Corral
#1, 301 Alta Ln
Brookings OR 97416
503-469-1969
(Buck Jones still lives!)

Classic Images
PO Box 809
301 E Third Ave
Muscatine IA 42761
319-263-2331
www.classicimages.com

Cliffhanger
Boyd Magers, Editor

1312 Stagecoach Road SE
Albuquerque NM 87123
(For fans of serials—awesome)

Cowboys and Indians
PO Box 2441
Cupertino CA 95015
www.cowboysandindians.com

Hoppy Talk
6310 Friendship Dr
New Concord OH 92624
(The only newsletter dedicated to Hopalong)

The Old Cowboy Picture Show
PO Box 66
Camden SC 29020
www.cowboyshow.com

Roy Rogers Riders Club
3950 Green Mountain RD
Branson MO 65616
417-339-1900
www.royrogers.com
(A resurrection of the original Riders Club)

*Roy Rogers/Dale Evans Collectors
   Association*
PO Box 1166
Portsmouth OH 45662-1166
614-353-0900

The Silver Bullet
PO Box 1493
Longmont CO 80502
303-485-9997
Theloneranger@worldnet.att.net
(Lone Ranger newsletter)

SPERDVAC *RadioGram*
(SPERDVAC: Society to Preserve
   and Encourage Radio Drama,
   Variety and Comedy)
PO Box 7177
Van Nuys CA 91409
(If you enjoy radio drama, this
   group is for you!)

Trail Dust
407 W Rosemary LN
Falls Church VA 22046
(Great source for information on
   TV cowboys)

Under Western Skies
104 Chestnut Dr
Waynesville NC 28786

Western Clippings
Boyd Magers, Editor
1312 Stagecoach Road SE
Albuquerque NM 87123
(The best source for news about
   TV and movie cowboys)

Western Revue
Bill Russell
404 Hermitage Dr
Altamonte Springs FL 32771

Wildest Westerns
1146 North Central Ave # 316
Glendale CA 91202
Fax: 818-247-0646
www.wildestwesterns.com

Wranglers Roost
23 Sabrina Way
Stoke Bishop, Bristol
BS9 1ST
England

New magazines and newsletters appear continually, so keep your eye on the newsstand and your ear to the ground.

3

They Went Thataway:
Web Links

With the advent of the computer age, the cyber corral can be quite crowded. There are hundreds of western themed Web sites on the Internet now, and more appear weekly. As with anything, some new sites are worth looking at, some not. I shall attempt to give a relatively short list of the "Best of the West" Net resources. The list is in alphabetical order.

www.abe.com
A good source for rare and out of print books. Abe.com has extensive listings for over 1,000,000 holdings in their affiliate stores.

www.accomics.com
Bill Black, the publisher of AC Comics, has long been a "B" Western fan and has contributed much to the genre. His reprint comics can be purchased online.

www.amazon.com
Next to eBay, Amazon carries the best selection of merchandise. Books, collectibles, and services are all sold on Amazon. Their search engine encompasses many sale sites such as Yahoo.com, eBay and used book dealers.

www.autry-museum.org
The official Web site of the Gene Autry Western Heritage Museum. Home to the gift shop, museum displays and other resources.

www.barnesandnoble.com
Barnes and Noble is a wonderful online bookstore. Dedicated to the best reference and fiction books available, B & N upholds its reputation for quality books, quality merchandise, quality service, and great prices.

www.bostonpete.com
Boston Pete is a great rail to tie your horse to! Jam-packed with nostalgia links to topics from riding to singing. Will Hutchins (Sugarfoot) hosts a regular Internet radio show on this cyber ranch.

www.celebhost.net
Clayton Moore, Guy Williams, Fess Parker and other stars receive trib-

ute on this celebrity domain. Each page has extensive links to current information.

www.cgccomics.com

In order to protect the comics industry from self-destruction, the CGC standard has evolved. CGC grading is done by an independent body guaranteeing an impartial grade and consequently improving the inherent value of key comics. Highly recommended for your prized comic books.

www.collectorsonline.com

This well-researched web page is your gateway to the world of fan clubs. Over 1100 clubs can be found on topics from A to Z. Contact information, mailing addresses, and web pages are listed in this valuable link.

www.comiclink.com

A highly respected Web site dedicated to the purchase, sale, swapping and certification of CGC comic books and comic book collectibles.

www.cowboypal.com

The most popular western Web site today. Joe Konnyu has done a masterful job of creating a tribute to the cowboy stars of his youth.

www.dccomics.com

The home page of DC Comics features information on upcoming comics and their entire lineup of publications (including *Mad Magazine*). Artist and writer profiles are also featured. An internet newsletter is available.

www.eBay.com

The best Web site is eBay. Ever since its innocent beginning several years ago, it has grown into the most comprehensive source for everything. If you want to sell or buy, check out eBay first. It has recently expanded to include Half Price.com and the eBay Stores concept.

www.eknifeworks.com

The home of Smoky Mountain Knife Works, a highly recommended knife and collectible distributor. Handling several lines, they are the place to go for your knife collecting needs.

www.employees.oxy.edu/jerry/index.html

Remember Monument Valley? If you have ever seen any John Wayne movie, and in the background a towering mountain looms, that is Monument Valley. This web page contains an extensive list of movie locations from Brazil to Canada. Pictures are included for your reference. Excellent for the film fan who loves trivia.

www.endeavorcomics.com/largent/lr1.html

Steve Largent's contribution to the Lone Ranger lore. The first Ranger page that inspired Mr. Jensen and Mr. Konnyu (www.cowboypal.com). A good Lone Ranger primer.

www.fiftiesweb.com

A great web page dedicated to the culture and cultural icons of the 1950s. Full of articles, links, and product histories. This page includes an excellent history of 1950s television and television history.

www.hakes.com

As home to the Hake Empire, this Web site gives you access to Hake auctions, consignments, and pricing information. Ted Hake is author of the *Official Hake's Price Guide to Character Toys.*

www.herbjeffries.com

The home web page of the first black western star. Also an accomplished jazz musician, he left his mark on Hollywood in the 1930s. A good place to learn about a true pioneer.

www.heritagecomics.com

Heritage Comics is unique in the comics industry. They hold an annual comics auction that has attracted incredible merchandise. Recently they have sold first issues of Batman, Superman, Wonder Woman, Action, and other key heroes of the Golden Age. Each auction's results are maintained in a database for future reference. If you need to sell your key issues, Heritage Comics can be a great help. If you are looking for key issues, look here first.

www.highnoon.com

High Noon auctions is the Sotheby's of the western world. They have an excellent reputation for honesty and integrity. Linda Kohn, one of the partners, is co-founder of the Gene Autry Western Heritage Museum. If you have high grade western collectibles, consider High Noon.

www.hopalong.com

The official Hopalong Cassidy Web site. Produced by the holders of the Hopalong copyright, this is the final authority on all things Hoppy.

www.howthewestwasfun.com

How the West was Fun carries a line of reproductions of Roy Rogers products originally marketed in the 1940s and 1950s. A great way to remember Roy, Trigger and Dale.

www.iguide.net

Iguide.net is an excellent source for the buyer and seller, designed as a resource to enable the collector to check both buying and selling prices online. It also allows the collector to maintain an online database. Filled with photographs and links to collectors' pages, it is the first and last place to check for accurate prices.

www.imdb.com

The Internet Movie Database comprehensively covers film actors, actresses, and entertainment professionals. Included in each person's file is a short biography, a listing of all television and movie appearances, contact information, and related links where applicable. The IMDB is a worthwhile source for accurate information.

www.kenpiercebooks.com

Ken Pierce, another western fan, offers his collection of western comic strip reprints for the aficionado. An amazing collection of strips.

www.kovels.com

Kovels is the best source for information on antiques. Their web page contains articles, an online price guide, a guide to fakes and marks, Internet yellow pages for antiques services and products, a newsletter sign-up, and a well-maintained directory of sources. Ralph and Terry are well respected and well versed in their specialty.

www.lofcom.com/nostalgia

A good Web site encompassing old time radio and book reviews, downloads, newsletters, mailing lists, radio logs, and links. Some nostalgia TV features are included as well.

www.Louislamour.com

The official Internet home of Louis L'Amour. As an authentic westerner and writer, Mr. L'Amour exemplified the best and worst of the frontier struggle in his work. The best source for all things Louis L'Amour.

www.marvelcomics.com

The home page of mighty Marvel Comics. New issues are previewed, and profiles of professionals can be found here. The publisher of *Kid Colt*, *The Ringo Kid*, and the *Two Gun Kid*, Marvel has recently published *The Rawhide Kid*, the latest western series.

www.mastronet.com

Relatively new to the world of collectible auctions, MastroNetInc has quickly made a name for themselves. Great for consignments, or just looking for the special something to fill the last hole in your collection, look here.

www.melodyranchstudio.com

Still in use as a movie studio, Melody Ranch was the home base for Gene Autry's films and hundreds of other westerns during the 1930s and 1940s. Privately owned, it opens to the public during the Annual Santa Clarita Cowboy Poetry and Music Festival.

www.members.tripod.com/~ ClaytonMoore/index.html

Steve Jensen's amazing tribute to Clayton Moore, aka the Lone Ranger. Packed with interviews and news items related to the masked man. This is the place to be.

www.milehighcomics.com

Mile High Comics is one of the most respected comics dealers in North America. Their Web site allows you to browse their inventory (complete with pictures), to check out their online comic book price guide, and to list your comics for sale on their site.

www.mxbookfinder.com

The ultimate source for used and rare books. Their database covers all of their associate stores. You can search by author, title, edition and price.

www.oldsundaycomics.com

Andy Mandura has assembled an amazing selection of Sunday comic pages. Relive your youth. The best source I have found.

www.otrsite.com

Old time radio: The phrase evokes myriad memories. This site offers an excellent variety of links, articles, and MP3 downloads for the radio fan.

www.peterbrown.tv

This Peter Brown site, hosted by Randy Saunders, is the home of all things Peter Brown. Excellent links to other celebrity sites.

www.pinkbanana.com/rex

The official Rex Allen Museum in Willcox, Arizona, offers this Rex Allen tribute, straight from the heart. This great museum keeps the Arizona Cowboy alive in our memories.

www.readthewest.com

A relatively new online magazine dedicated to western fiction, poems and features. An excellent site for western fans.

www.royrogers.com

An offshoot of the Roy Rogers and Dale Evans Museum, this site is maintained by the Rogers family. It features memorial pages for both Roy and Dale, fan lists, fan messages, and the Roy Rogers Gift shop. As the first cowboy in cyberspace, royrogers.com is the best source for authorized Rogers collectibles.

www.seeing-stars.com

An amazing reference page for the fan who enjoys Hollywood. The landscape, cultural locations, movie and TV studios, and the birth and death and worship places of the stars are presented in this all-inclusive, one-stop celebrity site.

www.series.net

For the collector of any juvenile series, the challenge is to find good information. This site is a great source for any series fan. The Hardy Boys, the Lone Ranger, and Nancy Drew can all be found here. Cover scans are included for reference purposes.

www.sperdvac.org

The official web page of the Society for Preservation and Encouragement of Radio Drama, Variety and Comedy is a good starting point in your search for information on the golden age of radio.

www.sothebys.com

The official Web site of Sotheby's Auction House. If you own items of extraordinary value, look to Sotheby's for your appraisals. Their tradition of excellence is unequaled.

www.surfnetinc.com/chuck/trio.htm

Chuck Anderson, the head wrangler at the Old Corral, manages this roundup of cowboy information. From Fred Thompson to Clint Eastwood, they are found here. A real treasure for the front row kid.

www.tonygill.co.uk/welcome.html

The official Robert Fuller Web site is a good way to learn about a television pioneer. From his early career to his latest work on Walker, it's all here.

www.vintagelibrary.com

An outstanding Web site featuring the best in classic fiction. With content ranging from science fiction to classic western authors, the library has e-books, old time radio downloads, themed pages, and much, much more.

www.westernmusic.org

The Western Music Association Web site, home to over 200 professional musicians from North America, offers booking information and support services for members. Great source for festival organizers.

www.yahoo.com

Yahoo offers browsers many features. One of the most useful is their special interest chat groups. If you search under a specific topic such as John Wayne, Roy Rogers or Gene Autry, you can find a group dedicated to that topic. Chats or news groups are an excellent way to get current information or just exchange stories. Highly recommended!

www.yesterdayland.com

Yesterdayland is the online home of nostalgia. Containing features on television shows, interviews with celebrities, and links with associated pages, Yesterdayland is an invaluable source for information on your favorite stars.

www.zorro.com

The official Web site of Zorro Productions, the copyright holder of Zorro. Home to information on the history, the movies, and the television hero known as Zorro. An online gift shop features rare Zorro items. News updates are also provided when available.

Throughout this book, you will find many other related Web sites. Chapter 6 lists useful Web sites for collectibles. Chapter 8 lists preservation-oriented Web sites. Other chapters also list sites pertinent to their topics.

The Internet is a big place, full of both information and misinformation. Research, compare, call or email an authority on your topic of interest. "Experts" are just professional fans who love to share their knowledge. Someday you, too, could be called an expert.

4

Cowboy Cultural Go-to-Meetin's: Museums

As the cowboy culture threatens to disappear in North America, collectors, curators and fans are joining forces to fight for the culture's preservation.

Once only the Smithsonian held cowboy and western cultural treasures within its vaults. Now the active western themed museums number over 100! There are museums dedicated to every aspect of cowboy culture. There are rodeo museums, movie museums, lifestyle museums, cultural icon museums, studio museums, and of course art and craft museums. This chapter lists the most prominent facilities.

Movie Legend Museums

Rex Allen Museum
1100 W Rex Allen Dr
Willcox AZ 85643
520-384-4583
www.pinkbanana.com/rex

The Rex Allen Museum, located in Rex's hometown of Willcox, Arizona, is home to the best collection of Rex Allen artifacts available. As you enter the first thing you encounter is Rex's beloved horse, Koko, raising his hooves in the air to welcome you to Rex's domain. Housing personal items and memorabilia from Rex's long film career, the Willcox Museum is a real pleasure.

Gene Autry Museum
PO Box 67
Gene Autry OK 73436
580-294-3047
www.cow-boy.com/museum.htm

Front view of the Rex Allen Museum in Willcox, Arizona. (Photograph courtesy Rex Allen Museum)

The Gene Autry Museum is housed in the former Gene Autry School in Gene Autry, Oklahoma, and is home to an outstanding collection of singing cowboy memorabilia featuring Roy Rogers, Gene Autry, Tex Ritter, Jimmy Wakely, Eddie Dean and others. Entry is free of charge, with donations accepted.

Autry Museum of Western Heritage
4700 Western Heritage Way
Los Angeles CA 90027-1432
323-667-2000
www.autry-musuem.org

The home of many fine collections, the Autry Museum of Western Heritage features more than a Gene Autry exhibit. It is home to a theater, a traveling exhibit area, a movie memorabilia section, and the western heritage collection. Displaying many priceless artifacts, the Western Heritage Museum gives you a glimpse into the past. James Nottage, head curator, has done a remarkable job of procuring, assembling and managing the very best of cowboy culture.

> William S. Hart Museum and Ranch
> 24151 San Fernando Rd
> Newhall CA 91321
> 661-254-4584
> www.hartmuseum.org

William S. Hart was one of the earliest stars in Hollywood. Starring in silent films, he made the transition to sound and into history. Renowned as a director, stuntman, writer and actor, he built his mansion in 1926 and left it to the county of Los Angeles upon his death. Mr. Hart collected authentic western art from Charlie Russell and Frederic Remington as well as movie props and memorabilia from his films. Various animals, including American bison, surround the ranch and provide activities for kids of all ages.

> Hopalong Cassidy Museum
> 15231 SW Parallel Rd
> Benton KS 67017
> 316-778-2121
> www.prairierosechuckwagon.com/hopalong_cassidy_
> museum_at_prair.htm

The Hopalong Cassidy Museum opened in August 2003, and this facility, hosted by the Prairie Rose Chuckwagon Supper Facility, is the official and only Hoppy museum in North America. It contains memorabilia, novels, posters, movie and TV stills, original films and television shows. A Hoppy theatre shows movies and television episodes as well. For the happy Hoppy fan, it's the real thing!

> Tom Mix Museum
> 721 N Delaware
> PO Box 190
> Dewey OK 74029
> 918-534-1555

The Tom Mix Museum houses Tom Mix's personal collection of movie memorabilia, books, and movies. It gives a glimpse into the life of one of Hollywood's earliest cowboy stars. For those old enough to remember his daring stunts and thrilling movies, it is a walk back in time. For the young, it is a personal tour across generations.

A bronze statue of Tex Ritter and White Flash greets visitors to the Tex Ritter Museum in Carthage, Texas. (Photograph courtesy Tex Ritter Museum)

Tex Ritter Museum
(Texas Country Music Hall of Fame)
1 W Panola St
Carthage TX 75633
903-693-6634
Fax 903-693-8578
www.carthagetexas.com

The Tex Ritter Museum is also home to the Texas Country Music Hall of Fame. Found in Carthage, Texas, this museum pays homage to Tex Ritter, Jim Reeves, and many other fine musicians. A larger-than-life bronze statue of Tex and White Flash greets you as you enter the museum.

Roy Rogers–Dale Evans Museum
3950 Green Mountain Rd
Branson MO 65616
417-339-1900
www.royrogers.com

As Dusty Rogers (Roy Rogers Jr.) often says, "Dad never threw anything out"—and we fans are very thankful for that! When you enter this

The Roy Rogers–Dale Evans Museum in Branson, Missouri. (Photograph courtesy the Rogers family)

museum, Trigger himself greets you as you pass through the gates, and from there, the spirits of Roy and Dale urge you on. The museum houses thousands of Roy Rogers items, including comics, trucks, hats, cups, family pictures, and even hunting trophies. To visit the museum is truly a treat not to be missed by any Roy Rogers fan. Onsite facilities include a gift shop, exhibits, and snack shop, and the museum is wheelchair accessible. Since the move from Victorville, California, to Branson, the museum now features interactive displays, a movie theater, a special area for young buckaroos, and a performance theater featuring the Rogers family musical acts.

Will Rogers Memorial Museum
1720 W Will Rogers Blvd
Claremore OK 74017
918-341-719
800-324-9455
www.willrogers.com

The Will Rogers Museum is full of Will Rogers history. Donated to the town of Claremore by his widow and family after Rogers' untimely passing, this museum pays homage to Will Rogers' life as a writer, trick roper, vaudeville performer, movie star, and homespun philosopher. The research wing contains over 18,000 photographs, letters, manuscripts, and contracts, and well over 2,000 volumes pertaining to life during the period 1875–1935. This museum is affiliated with the Will Rogers homestead at Oologah. Both sites offer much for the Will Rogers aficionado.

> Will Rogers State Historic Park
> 14523 Sunset Blvd
> Pacific Palisades CA 90272
> 310-454-8212
> www.parks.ca.gov

The home of humorist Will Rogers is preserved in this 186-acre state park located off Sunset Boulevard. His 31-room ranch house, riding stables, full-sized polo field, and hiking trails are all maintained as they were in the '20s and '30s. This historic park also functions as a working ranch, complete with full equestrian facilities.

> John Wayne and War Museum
> Findley Lake Trading Company
> North Rd
> Findley NY 14736
> 716-769-6690

A new entry into the world of American museums, the John Wayne and War Museum is privately operated. This museum has a collection of John Wayne memorabilia ranging from comic books to actual movie props (Alamo toupee and standup), as well as assorted authentic war items. This small museum is sure to please. The Findley Lake Trading Company operates a John Wayne themed gift shop to satisfy even the most discriminating fan.

Art Museums

> Amon Carter Museum
> 3501 Camp Bowie Blvd
> Fort Worth TX 76107-2695
> 817-738-1933
> www.cartermuseum.org

The Amon Carter Museum was established through the generosity of Amon Carter (1879–1955) to house his collection of American art. In the recently renovated facility, works by Frederic Remington, C. M. Russell,

Rockwell Kent, John Singer Sargeant, Will Barnet, Stuart Davis, Hiram Powers; photographs by William Jackson and Robert Adams; and works on paper by William Johnson, Maud Squire, and Peter Rindisbacher are displayed.

Cowboy Artists of America Museum
1550 Bandera Hwy
Kerrville TX 78025
830-896-2553
www.caamuseum.com
www.americanwesternart.org

Located in the heart of Hill Country, the Cowboy Artists of America Museum features the best of contemporary cowboy and western artists and the pioneers of yesterday. Over 25 artists, including John Hampton, Joe Beeler, Charlie Dye, and George Phippen, are highlighted in this outstanding collection housed in a fortressed hacienda. This museum is recommended for western art enthusiasts everywhere.

Eiteljorg Museum
500 W Washington
Indianapolis IN 46204
317-636-WEST
www.eiteljorg.org

The Eiteljorg Museum is unique. From its distinctive architecture, inspired by the land and people of the American Southwest, to its vast holdings of both Native American and western art, the museum serves to dispel historic and modern day stereotypes of America's native peoples.

Fred Harman Art Museum
(Red Ryder and Little Beaver)
2560 W Hwy 160
PO Box 192
Pagosa Springs CO 81147
www.toski.com/fredharman/index.html

The Fred Harman Art Museum features painting of Red Ryder, Little Beaver, and many other characters who lived in Mr. Harman's fertile imagination. The studio features three galleries of artwork and displays including original artwork, paintings, and western memorabilia from his own collection. This museum is a real jewel for the Red Ryder fan.

Billboard welcoming visitors to the Fred Harman Art Museum. (Used with permission of the museum)

National Museum of Wildlife Art
2820 Rungius Rd
PO Box 6825
Jackson Hole WY 83001
307-733-5771
800-313-9553
www.wildlifeart.org

The National Museum of Wildlife Art, located three miles north of Jackson Hole, Wyoming, is a fitting tribute both to the nation's wildlife and to the artists who have portrayed it. Nestled in a hillside that overlooks the National Elk Reserve, this museum houses nearly 2300 works of art celebrating wildlife in its natural habitat.

Frederic Remington Art Museum
303 Washington St
Ogdensburg NY 13669
313-393-2425
www.fredericremington.org

The world's finest collection of the art of Frederic Remington, the great nineteenth century artist who vividly depicted the *real* Old West, is housed here at the Frederic Remington Art Museum. Also including everything from scrapbooks, notes, and photographs to Remington's furniture and even his cigars, the depth and breadth of the holdings are unmatched. The full scope of Remington's talent can be found here, from his awe-inspiring portraits to his bronze work. For a full examination of Remington, there is nowhere else to go.

C. M. Russell Museum
400 13th St N
Great Falls MT 59401
406-727-8787
www.cmrussell.org

The C. M. Russell Museum is home to the Charlie Russell archives. Recently renovated, the museum now contains almost 80,000 square feet and occupies a full city block. Boasting Mr. Russell's log cabin as an exhibit, it also houses 14 galleries, each presenting different aspects of his work. Encompassing his bronze works, pen and paper work, oil paintings and charcoals, the facility also presents work by O. C. Seltzer, historical photographers, and many contemporaries of Mr. Russell. Charlie Russell's work, which captured the essence of the west with all of its varied flavors, today helps us remember the fading frontier.

Museums of Indian Art and Life

Desert Caballeros Museum
21 N Frontier St
Wickenburg AZ 85390
928-684-2272
www.westernmuseum.org

The Desert Caballeros Museum is a treasure. Its exhibits include a changing selection from a collection of over 400 works from various artists; the "Spirit of the Cowboy" collection which includes everything from saddles to chaps dating from the 1870s to the 1950s; a gem and mineral display; an early Arizona street scene; and an outstanding history diorama. This museum displays the real West in "western" and leaves you longing for more.

Heard Museum
2301 N Central Ave
Phoenix AZ 85004
602-252-8840
www.heard.org

The Heard Museum was founded by Dwight B. and Maie Bartlett Heard in 1929 to house their personal collection of cultural and fine art. Its mission is to educate the public about the heritage and the living cultures and arts of native peoples, emphasizing the Southwest. Temporary and permanent displays feature prominent cultural movements of the past and present.

Hubbard Museum of the American West
841 Highway 70 W
PO Box 40
Ruidoso Downs NM 88346
505-378-4142
www.zianet.com/museum

The Hubbard Museum of the American West is an important part of Ruidoso history. Located next to the Ruidso Racetrack, it pays homage to the racing greats in New Mexico. Originally the Anne C. Stradling collection, the Hubbard Museum has added the Racehorse Hall of Fame to its amazing collection of bits, spurs, bridles, saddles and artifacts, carriages, wagons, and horse-drawn vehicles from around the world. The Hubbard Museum is the only New Mexico museum accepted into the Smithsonian Affiliate Program.

Mashantucket Pequot Museum
110 Pequot Tr
PO Box 3180
Mashantucket CT 06339-3180
800-411-9671
www.mashantucket.com

The Mashantucket Pequot Museum is amazing, utilizing realistic dioramas, interactive computer displays, 3D graphics, film and video to present the rich and diverse cultural heritage of the Pequots from prehistoric times to the present. The exhibits include a half-acre Pequot village, stunningly displayed archaeological artifacts, and many interactive learning tools for all ages. The Pequot is truly a museum that reflects the past for the sake of the future.

Museum of Indian Arts and Culture
PO Box 2087
Sante Fe NM 87504
505-476-1256

The Museum of Indian Arts and Culture is unique. Coupled with the Laboratory of Anthropology, it is suited to serve as both an educational and research facility. As part of New Mexico's Office of Cultural Affairs and their affiliate museums, it has a scope that goes beyond art. The Indian culture of various periods is represented through various media, and interesting lessons are taught in an engaging fashion. Home to an impressive permanent display, it also hosts unique traveling exhibits.

Museum of the Cherokee Indian
Hwy 441 & Drama Rd
PO Box 1599
Cherokee NC 28719
828-497-3481
www.cherokeemuseum.org

Take a trip through time. A Cherokee storyteller greets you and leads you through the Paleo era, the Archaic era, and the time of Selu and Atlatls. A chieftain meets you during the Woodland and Mississipian period and leads you to the present, where photographic images of Ostenaco, Cunne Shote, and Woytl are preserved. The Trail of Tears takes you back in time as it draws you on through the museum. The Museum of the Cherokee Indian incorporates modern technology and drama to leave you with an appreciation of a people of history.

Panhandle-Plains Museum
2401 4th Ave
Canyon TX 79015
806-651-2244
www.wtamu/museum/home

The Panhandle-Plains Museum has grown since Hattie Anderson first envisioned the Historical Society in 1921. She stated in 1921 that it would be the society's "sacred duty ... to collect the record of life here and hand this on to the children of the future." This vision is still alive and thrives in the museum. The one million artifacts from New Mexico and Texas include a replica Pioneer Town and an engaging native history exhibit. The Panhandle-Plains Museum will increase your appreciation of the past and its pioneers.

Millicent Rogers Museum
PO Box Station A
Taos, New Mexico 87571
505-758-2462
www.millicentrogers.org

Known to the world as an American beauty and fashion icon, Millicent Rogers helped preserve southwestern native cultures through her own designs and collection. Housing thousands of pieces of native and contemporary jewelry as well as art from tapestries to canvases and clothing, this exceptional museum presents a fascinating look at native cultures and their lasting influence.

Western Culture/Lifestyle Museums

Billy the Kid Museum
1601 E Sumner Ave
Fort Sumner NM 88119
505-355-2380
www.billythekidmuseum.net

As one of the most colorful characters of the American West, Billy the Kid lives on as a legend. The holdings of the Billy the Kid Museum include his rifle, chaps and spurs, hair, wanted posters, and books, along with other items such as antique firearms, and automobiles. Privately owned, this museum has been thrilling young and old for over 45 years, and shows no signs of stopping!

Boot Hill Museum
Front Street
Dodge City, KS 67801
1-800-OLDWEST
www.boothill.org

The Boot Hill Museum was founded in 1947 to collect, preserve, and interpret the history of Dodge City in the 1870s. The exhibits include reconstructed buildings and businesses of the period. An interpretive program gives visitors a glimpse into the town's history when it served as a buffalo traders' center and later on, a cattle town. The town's history is reflected in photographs, documents, objects, and recreated events.

Buffalo Bill Historical Center
720 Sheridan Ave
Cody WY 82414-3428

307-587-4771
www.bbhc.org

The Buffalo Bill Historical Center houses four world class museums: the Buffalo Bill Museum, the Whitney Gallery of Western Art, the Plains Indian Museum, and the Cody Firearms Museum. The BBHC looks respectfully at the past, with an understanding of the present and an eye to the future. The Buffalo Bill Museum examines and presents the life of Bill Cody, showman and frontier rider. Of additional interest, the Firearms Museum presents an overview of firearms in history.

The Cowboy Memorial and Library
40371 Cowboy Lane
Caliente CA 93518
661-867-2410
www.tehachapi.com/cowboy/

Paul de Fonville has assembled an amazing collection of western artifacts and scholarly resources. Located near the entrance to the Sequoia National Park, this museum includes both inside and outside exhibits designed to educate visitors on the cowboy way of life. Authentic artifacts number in the thousands, and many wear marks from trail use. For a real cowboy experience, Paul will be glad to help.

Glenbow Museum
130-9th Ave SE
Calgary, Alberta, Canada T2G 0P3
403-268-4100
www.glenbow.org

The Glenbow Museum was created in 1966 by the bequeathment of Eric Harvie's vast collection to the people of Alberta. Today, the Glenbow's collection of over 1,000,000 artifacts is housed in a 93,000 square foot facility. Encompassing many cultures and time frames, the Glenbow also serves as the premier research facility for historians. Alberta's history, from dinosaurs to ranchers to oil men, is presented for all posterity.

The Las Vegas City Museum and
Rough Riders Memorial Collection
725 Grand Ave
Las Vegas NV 87701
505-425-8726
www.moravalley.com/lv-mus/

In 1898, America helped the Cuban people gain independence from Spain. The Rough Riders, a volunteer cavalry, consisted of cowboys from the west. Theodore Roosevelt, then secretary of the navy, was second in command. This museum consists of personal artifacts and mementos of the Rough Riders, photographs, and even the uniforms of the Rough Riders themselves.

The Museum of the Big Bend
Sul Ross State University
Box C-101
Alpine TX 79832
915-837-8143
www.sulross.edu/~museum/

The Museum of the Big Bend represents the cultural diversity of the Big Bend area. With a history reaching back thousands of years, the American Indians left their mark on the land. The Spaniards, with their system of missions and presidios, imprinted their unique culture on the native Indians, only to be replaced by the Mexican nation. Later still, the expanding United States added another element to the character of the area. The museum holds prehistoric items, Texas trappings, and the "Livermore Cache." For the real Texas story, come to the Big Bend.

The Museum of Northern Arizona
3101 N Fort Valley Rd
Flagstaff AZ 86001
928-774-5213
www.musnaz.org

Located in the "gateway to the Colorado Plateau," the Museum of Northern Arizona encourages a broader understanding of the unique beauty and character of its land and people. Containing exhibits ranging from native culture to dinosaurs, from science to prehistoric peoples, this museum is the only nationally accredited northern Arizona facility.

Museum of Northwest Colorado
590 Yampa Ave
Craig CO 81625
970-824-6360
www.museumnwco.org

The Museum of Northwest Colorado is an adventure. Presenting true stories to their visitors on a regular basis, this facility boasts an extensive

The National Cowboy and Western Heritage Museum in Oklahoma City, Oklahoma. (Photograph courtesy of the museum)

collection of pioneer and western artifacts. For a taste of Colorado history, you can't go wrong here.

> National Cowboy and Western Heritage Museum
> 1700 NE 63rd St
> Oklahoma City OK 73111
> 405-478-2250
> www.nationalcowboymuseum.org

Aptly named, this world class facility focuses primarily on cowboy heritage. Housing galleries such as the American Cowboy, American Rodeo, Children's Cowboy Corral, the Joe Grandee Museum of the Frontier West, Prosperity Junction, the Weitzenhoffer Fine Arms Gallery and the End of the Trail, this museum is a true treasure.

> National Cowgirl Museum and Hall of Fame
> 1720 Gendy St
> Fort Worth TX 76107
> 817-336-4475
> www.cowgirl.net

Mural from the National Cowgirl Museum in Fort Worth, Texas. (Photograph courtesy of the museum)

The National Cowgirl Museum and Hall of Fame is the only museum dedicated to the women who exemplified the pioneer way of life. Started in 1975 in Hereford, this museum has recently expanded to its present location to increase its national profile. Currently celebrating 159 women from Narcissa Prentiss Whitman (first women pioneer to cross the Rockies), to Dale Evans Rogers, to artist Georgia O'Keeffe, the museum seeks to honor women of spirit, courage, and leadership.

The Nelson Museum of the West
1714 Carey Ave
Cheyenne, Wyoming 82001
307-635-7670
www.nelsonmuseum.com

"Preserving the Past for the Future" is the motto of this private museum located in Cheyenne, Wyoming. It holds such exhibits as worldwide wildlife trophies, Plains Indian and Pueblo Indian artifacts, a U.S. Cavalry room, cowboy and Indian weapons, cowboy and cowgirl clothing, and an exceptional Edward Bohlin display. A significant collection of rodeo and cowboy and Indian artifacts makes up the majority of the holdings.

Pony Express Museum
914 Penn St
St Joseph MO 64503
816-279-5059
www.ponyexpress.org

The Pony Express Museum pays tribute to a fascinating part of American history. From April 1860 to October 1861, the express carried mail from St. Joseph, Missouri, to Sacramento, California. Housing rider essentials such as saddlebags and personal effects, the museum is educational and entertaining.

Pro Rodeo Hall of Fame and
Museum of the American Cowboy
Rodeo Dr
Colorado Springs CO
719-528-4764
www.prorodeo.com

The Pro Rodeo Hall of Fame and Museum of the American Cowboy is the best link to the rodeo way of life. The rodeo is an entertainment with roots in real life. Devoted exclusively to the sport of rodeo and the men and women who made it great, the museum treats visitors to a world class presentation of video, audio, and history.

The Texas Ranger Museum and Hall of Fame
PO Box 2570
Waco TX 76702-2570
254-750-8631
www.texasranger.org

A real part of the American West as well as a movie legend, the Texas Rangers have a long and storied history. In 1976, the Texas Ranger Museum and Hall of Fame was designated the Rangers' official museum. Built on the site of an 1839 Texas Ranger encampment, this facility includes an outstanding collection of Ranger artifacts. The Texas Rangers Museum is a great place to learn an important part of the Texas story.

The Wyoming State Museum
Barrett Building
2301 Central Ave
Cheyenne WY 82002
307-777-7022
http://wyomuseum.state.wy.us

The Wyoming State Museum is a treasure house. Telling the story of Wyoming from its prehistoric past to the present, it gives the participant an encompassing view. Exhibits include "Swamped with Coal," "The Wild Bunch," the upcoming "Living in Wyoming," and artifacts covering all genres. The "Wild West" period of Wyoming is well represented in this splendid facility.

Wells Fargo Museums
Various locations
www.wellsfargohistory.com/museums/

The Wells Fargo Museums are the real thing. In all six museums you can find real gold nuggets, real stagecoaches, and more. Located in San Francisco, San Diego, Sacramento, Old Sacramento, Los Angeles, Minneapolis, Portland, and Anchorage, the museums do an excellent job of presenting a fascinating history. The Wells Fargo Line is tied closely to the story of the west and its expansion. Carrying cargo, pioneers, and culture from east to west, Wells Fargo formed the backbone of growth. Enjoy free admission to these authentic exhibits that turn back the hands of time.

Toy/Collectible Museums

Fawcett Antique Toy Museum
Famous Fine Art and Antiques
Box 1156
3506 Route 1
Waldoboro ME 04572
207-832-7398
http://home.gwi.net/~fawcetoy/

The Fawcett Antique Toy Museum is the best toy museum, period. The displays boast antique toys of all kinds. Included in this museum's archives are radio premiums, cereal boxes, character radios, puppets, guitars, original comic book artwork, books, the Brace Beemer Lone Ranger guns, a Gene Autry rodeo saddle, various pieces of clothing worn by film cowboys like Roy Rogers and Rex Allen, WXYZ memorabilia ranging from artwork that hung in the studio to scripts and props, and so much more. If you love toys—if you really, *really* love toys—this is the place to be young again.

End Note

The list above represents only a few of the many museums dedicated to the cowboy and western lifestyle. Furthermore, the job of preserving the past through historical societies and museums is not finished. As the 21st century meets us head on with the challenges of technology vs. environment, we have to look to the past for the key to our survival.

All throughout North America, museums and societies seek to preserve the past. It is our duty, as responsible citizens, to learn from these resources, to be a participant in their successes, so the lessons of the past will not be lost.

For an excellent web resource for world class museums, check out:

http:// 123world.com/museumsandgalleries/index.html

and

http://www.askart.com/

(for dedicated art museums)

5

"Say, Do You Know Where to Find...?" Books for Reference and Research

One of the biggest thrills for the collector is finding a great book. There's nothing like sitting down with a book about your favorite star and losing yourself in it. There have been many good books published over the years, and some great ones in recent memory.

When reading books on the entertainment industry, it is important to remember that even the most careful researchers must sometimes rely on the memories of people in that industry, and memories cannot always be trusted. Roy Rogers told several variations of Trigger story over his lifetime; which one was true really doesn't matter. For most fans, what matters is not how much Roy paid for Trigger or when he purchased him, but the simple fact that Trigger was part of the Roy Rogers mystique, and that Trigger himself had many fans. The story of the creation of the Lone Ranger, too, has its many versions depending on the source.

As the era of a star's early career becomes increasingly distant, researchers are forced to rely upon secondary sources: children and their memories, studio information, co-stars, supporting players and finally, hearsay. Now that all but a few of the early stars have passed on, authors look to the stars and supporting players of the mid–1940s to late 1960s for information.

As a result, we are seeing fewer volumes based on firsthand information, and erroneous material is commonly represented as fact. The death of Buck Jones was called a "heroic" act, but in reality, he may have been under a table passed out. History is often rewritten for the faint of heart.

But to one who loves Buck Jones, the Buck Jones books by Buck Rainey are a treasure. To one who loves Hopalong Cassidy, the Clarence Mulford story and the films of Hopalong Cassidy are a treat. Not all the books listed here will appeal to every reader, but there should be at least a little something for everyone.

The following list is only a guideline. I will not list all of the books published that fans everywhere have adored and turned into dog-eared bibles, but only the best of the best, the most loved of the loved and some of my favorites. I will list them in several categories, such as biographies, price guides, and more. Where possible I have listed publisher, year of release, and length. Contact information for the publishers (where available) is listed at the end of this chapter. If it is out of print, you may have to purchase a basic through www.amazon.com, or eBay or an online used bookstore.

Biographies

GENE AUTRY

Back in the Saddle Again. Gene Autry and Mickey Herskowitz. Doubleday, 1978. Hardcover, 252 pages.

Gene Autry tells his life story with the help of Mickey Herskowitz. From his early days as a telegraph agent and his subsequent "discovery," Gene traces his career to the end of his public life in 1956. Building his business empire from his entertainment roots took over as he became a leading sports producer and investment entrepreneur. An extensive appendix includes a filmography and discography.

The Gene Autry Book. David Rothel. Empire, 1998. Hardcover, 294 pages.

Includes a giant, comprehensive collection of questions and answers, memorable quotes from Gene on a variety of subjects, a complete filmography, a discography, a listing of the 91 Gene Autry TV episodes and much more. A must-have for the Gene Autry fan!

LONE RANGER/CLAYTON MOORE

His Typewriter Grew Spurs. Fran Striker Jr. University of California Press, 1985.

Fran Striker Junior grew up to the sound of the pounding keys of his father, Fran Striker, the creator of the Lone Ranger. The younger Striker's memories, as presented in this book, of his father give us a fascinating look at the early days of the masked man, the Green Hornet, and his father's other creations.

I Was That Masked Man. Clayton Moore with Frank Thompson. Taylor, 1996. Hardcover and softcover.

Fans waited a long time for this one, but it was worth it. Clayton Moore finally tells his story. Frank Thompson does a great job and Clayton moves his mask down a little bit to give us a glimpse of his real life, demonstrating that he can be as engaging on paper as he was in person. This book is a must-have for the Lone Ranger fan. It offers a detailed appendix that includes Moore's filmography, a listing of all Lone Ranger episodes (even with John Hart), and a short Lone Ranger chronology.

TOM MIX

Tom Mix: A Heavily Illustrated Biography of the Western Star, with a Filmography. Paul Mix. McFarland, 2001. Hardcover, 336 pages.

Written by Tom Mix's grandson, this volume presents the most complete Tom Mix story written. Blending family sources with press releases and "Mix-ology," this book presents a good picture of the Tom Mix we never knew. Complete with family and publicity photos and a filmography, this volume is guaranteed to please any Mix fan.

The Tom Mix Book. M. G. "Bud" Norris. World of Yesterday. Softcover, 379 pages.

Covering Tom Mix's career from his circus days to his Hollywood life and everything in between, M. G. Norris gives us a picture of the phenomenon that Tom Mix became. Including his movie work (336 pages), his radio work, his circus career, toys, arcade items and much more, this book is an authoritative work on all things Tom Mix.

ROY ROGERS, DALE EVANS AND TRIGGER

Happy Trails. Roy Rogers, Dale Evans, and Jane and Michael Stern. Simon & Schuster, 1994. Hardcover, 252 pages.

Written in six parts, this charming autobiography of Roy and Dale can't help but touch you. You come away from this book realizing how lucky the youth of America were to have had the Rogers' influence in their lives. Roy and Dale alternate chapters, while Jane and Michael Stern write a short introduction to each section. Full of innocence, just like you'd expect.

Roy Rogers. Robert W. Phillips. McFarland, 1995. Hardcover, 446 pages.

The most complete Roy Rogers book ever written. Encompassing his personal, professional, merchandising, and recording lives, it leaves little out. For the dedicated Roy Rogers fan, its encyclopedic scope is priceless. For the lover of B Westerns, it breathes humanity into our image of Roy riding the range on Trigger, bringing justice where it was needed.

Trigger Remembered. William Witney. Earl Blair, 1989. Softcover, 78 pages.

In the only horse biography, William Witney thrills us with stories of the "Smartest Horse in the Movies." Acknowledged as one of the men who knew Trigger best, he fills in the gaps for the rest of us.

OTHER COWBOYS

Rex Allen: Arizona Cowboy. Bob Carman and Dan Scapperotti. Self published, 1982. Softcover, 96 pages.

The last of the singing cowboys, Rex Allen, is profiled in this Carman and Scapperotti volume. From Rex Allen's beginnings as a rodeo star to his breakout performances on the *Old Barn Dance*, his rise to fame is chronicled as are his later years as a Disney narrator. This book is illustrated with movie posters, publicity shots, and rare photos. Includes a filmography covering his television show *Frontier Doctor*; his movie roles; and his voiceover work for Disney. The only Allen biography available, this is a must-have for the Rex Allen fan.

James Arness: An Autobiography. James Arness and James E. Wise Jr. McFarland, 2001. Hardcover, 248 pages.

James Arness, in this autobiography, gives a spellbinding account of his life before, during and after *Gunsmoke* (1955–1975). Portraying Marshall Matt Dillon on *Gunsmoke* made his career, but his life was full before that. He was a soldier, producer, actor, and now devotes his time to charity work. This is a rare look at a man who changed the face of television.

Roy Barcroft: King of the Badmen. Bobby Copeland. Empire, 2000. Softcover, 168 pages.

If Roy Rogers was the ultimate white hat, then Roy Barcroft was the ultimate black-hat villain. Bobby Copeland has produced a landmark volume on this great character actor. Included in this book is his detailed biography, Barcroft's filmography, personal comments from his co-workers, the story of how he selected the name Roy, and his own words. A rare book on this amazing actor.

A Company of Heroes: My Life as an Actor in the John Ford Stock Company. Harry Carey Jr. Scarecrow, 1994. Hardcover, 218 pages.

Harry Carey Jr. learned his craft at the feet of two masters: Harry Carey Sr. and John Ford. His father, Harry Carey Sr., was a star, stuntman, and director, and an innovator in the stunt industry. Harry Carey Jr. has had a long career in the movies (recently starring with Tom Selleck), and this book recounts the highlights and low points during his journey. Harry Carey Jr. presents a well-written, entertaining volume complete with index and photographs.

The Western Films of Sunset Carson. Bob Carman and Dan Scapperotti. Self published, 1981. Softcover, 72 pages.

The only book produced on Sunset Carson, this edition reveals a side of Sunset that we never knew. As one of the first convention guests, Sunset thrilled many fans for years. This book includes a filmography and rare photographs. Find one if you can; it's worth the search.

Written, Produced and Directed: The Autobiography of Oliver Drake. Oliver Drake. Outlaw, 1990. Hardcover, 154 pages.

The complete story of Oliver Drake's life, from his cowboy roots to his roles as writer (music and script), director and producer at Republic Studios. Known for his directorial reign on *The Lone Ranger,* he also contributed behind the scenes (uncredited) to many other classic serials. This book sets the record straight on his influence on the art form called the serial. The text is supplemented by black and white photos and reproductions of movie posters. A recommended read on a great director.

Bill Elliot: The Peaceable Man. Bobby Copeland. Empire, 2000. Softcover, 192 pages.

From the foreword by Peggy Stewart to the last page, this book breaks new ground for serious Bill Elliot fans. Including sections on his comic books, his personal life, his obituary, his sidekicks, his filmography, his horses, and personal comments from those that knew him, this book gives you a full picture of the Bill Elliot we all admire.

John Ford: Hollywood's Old Master (The Oklahoma Western Biographies Volume 10). Ronald L. Davis. University of Oklahoma Press, 1997. Softcover, 400 pages.

John Ford, the master director, was responsible for many western classics. From *The Iron Horse* to his movement towards television, his work evolved. *Stagecoach* (1939) introduced us to John Wayne and demonstrated John Ford's brilliant casting. This book overflows with original research (from interviews) and insight into Ford's scarred psyche. A fascinating book profiling a monumental director.

William S. Hart: My Life East and West. William S. Hart. Houghton Mifflin, 1929, and R . R. Donnelley, 1994. Hardcover, 363 and 417 pages.

William S. Hart was one the true pioneers of the film industry. Arriving in Hollywood in 1913, he quickly rose through the ranks and became a leading writer, director, actor and producer of authentic westerns during the silent era. This autobiography recounts his early years and his friendships with Wyatt Earp, Wild Bill Hickock, and Bat Masterson. This book gives us a unique look at the beginning of westerns as we know them.

George "Gabby" Hayes, the Royal Jester of the B Westerns. Mario De Marco. Self Published. Softcover, 100 pages.

De Marco, veteran writer, convention organizer, western comic artist and western fan extraordinaire, has produced the only book about our favorite sidekick, Gabby Hayes. Trained as a classical actor, George Hayes went from stage, to westerns as sidekick to John Wayne, Hopalong Cassidy, and Roy Rogers, and then to his own television show. Always just a sidekick, he will always be remembered. Rare photos and illustrations by Mario De Marco supplement this charming book. De Marco has authored 35 books on B westerns and continues to delight readers of all ages.

Tim Holt. David Rothel. Empire, 1984. Hardcover, 285 pages.

This well-written book is a treasure trove for Tim Holt information. Containing childhood photos, film reviews, newspaper articles, his obituary, interviews from film magazines from the 1950s and with family members, this book is magnificent in its scope and coverage. From the front "painting" to the excellent print and photographic reproductions to the solid research and compilation efforts by David Rothel, this book comes highly recommended.

The Life and Films of Buck Jones: The Silent Era. Buck Rainey. World of Yesterday, 1988. Softcover.

Buck Jones was a major star during the silent era in Hollywood. With information culled from his widow, Buck Jones' family, and "Doc" Buck Rainey's research, this book is the most complete Buck Jones biography available. Complete with rare photos from the author's collection as well as the Jones family, this book is a treat.

The Life and Films of Buck Jones: The Sound Era. Buck Rainey. World of Yesterday. Softcover.

A followup to the silent era volume listed above. Focuses on Buck Jones' sound era career. Photos from the family and the author's collection supplement this useful book.

Allan "Rocky" Lane: Republic's Action Ace. Chuck Thornton, David Rothel. Empire, 1990. Hardcover, 181 pages.

A rare book about Allan "Rocky" Lane. David Rothel and Chuck Thornton have done an exemplary job. From Lane's earliest appearance to his role as the mystery voice of Mr. Ed, this book tells his tale in a riveting fashion.

Lash LaRue: The King of the Black Whip. Chuck Thornton, David Rothel. Empire, 1988. Softcover, 160 pages.

Lash LaRue was certainly one of a kind. As an actor, his career peaked in the 1940s and early 1950s, and his movies drew crowds. He used his whip as his primary weapon, and his appeal was his difference. His life, as told in this book, was as intriguing as his movies. A rare book on an unusual character in the history of the westerns.

The Clarence E. Mulford Story. Bernard A. Drew. Scarecrow, 1991. Hardcover, 307 pages.

Hopalong Cassidy (as remembered today) and the original hero (as conceived by Clarence E. Mulford) are not the same. This book examines the original prose works and compares them to the radio, movie, newspaper, and comic book versions as portrayed and reflected in William Boyd. Extensive lists of the original stories, books, movies, television shows, and tie in-merchandise are included to supplement the text.

Bob Nolan: A Biographical Guide and Annotations. Lawrence Hopper. Self Published, 2002. Hardcover, 96 pages.

As one of the original members of the Sons of the Pioneers, Bob Nolan has left his mark on popular music. In this book, Lawrence Hopper gives us a short biography with new information, a complete sessionography, and maps showing significant places in Bob Nolan's life. Originally published in a limited run of 500 copies, this book cries out for space on your bookshelf.

Tex Ritter: America's Most Beloved Cowboy. Bill O'Neal. Eakins, 1998. Softcover, 165 pages.

A well researched and written volume on the life and times of Tex Ritter. Covering his Broadway, radio, movie, television and recording life, this book will answer many questions about this popular cowboy.

The Sons of the Pioneers. Bill O'Neal, Fred Goodwin. Eakins, 2001. Softcover.

The Sons of the Pioneers are a national treasure. Recently celebrating 59 years in the entertainment industry, the Sons have included Roy Rogers, Bob Nolan, Tim Spencer, Ken Curtis, Lloyd Perryman, Hugh and Karl Farr, and others in their membership. This book, written by longtime associate Fred Goodwin, is an extensive history, filmography, discography and memorabilia listing of our favorite sons.

Bob Steele: His Reel Women. Bob Nareau. Bob Nareau Publications. Softcover, 177 pages.

An A–Z listing of Bob Steele's female leading stars. This book comes with complete with photos. Great trivia for the Bob Steele fan.

Those B-Western Cowboy Heroes Who Rode the Hollywood Range with Bob Steele. Bob Nareau. Bob Nareau Publications. Softcover, 183 pages.

The companion book to *His Reel Women*, this edition features a mini biography and sketch by Mr. Nareau of the male co-stars that shared the screen with Bob Steele.

Bob Steele: Stars and Support Players 1921 to 1946. Bob Nareau. Bob Nareau Publications. Softcover, 102 pages.

A must-have for the Bob Steele fan. This excellent book lists the more than 600 onscreen characters that Bob Steele rode against and battled with in his onscreen performances. Bob Nareau, the best Bob Steele historian today, includes rare photos in this volume.

Peggy Stewart: Princess of the Prairie. Bob Carman and Dan Scapperotti. Softcover, 176 pages.

Peggy Stewart has had an amazing career. Starring with Roy Rogers, Gene Autry and other stars, she has contributed much to the classic westerns we all love. In this Carman and Scapperotti book, we learn much more about this "princess," and leave wanting more. Complete with photos and filmography, this volume is a treasure.

More Than a Cowboy: The Life and Films of Fred Thompson and Silver King. Edgar M. Wyatt. Wyatt Classics, 1988. Hardcover.

Fred Thompson is no longer the forgotten cowboy. One of the early silent western stars, he "held court" during the 1920s. A former minister, he left his mark on the industry and movie fans everywhere. This book is the only complete biography of this western pioneer. Including more than 300 illustrations, letters, clippings, family memories and rare photos, this volume is a treasure.

Geo. W. Trendle: Creator and Producer of the Lone Ranger, the Green Hornet, Sgt. Preston, the American Agent, and Other Successes. Mary Bickel. Exposition, 1998. Hardcover, 193 pages.

George Washington Trendle was amazingly successful. From his early days as a theater owner in Los Angeles to his tenure as the producer and perhaps creator of the Lone Ranger, Green Hornet, Sgt. Preston, and other heroic characters, he pushed ahead with vigor and a keen business sense. The "Miser of Tinseltown" was responsible for the early development of Hollywood and its present location. An informative book about a fascinating man, *Geo. W. Trendle* is a must-have for any radio/movie fan.

John Wayne ... There Rode a Legend: A Western Tribute. Jane Pattie, Wilma Russell, Maureen O'Hara. Eakin, 2001. Hardcover, 274 pages.

This superbly illustrated coffee table book highlights the life, career, and memories of John Wayne, American. With a foreword by Maureen O'Hara, this tome is invaluable to the serious John Wayne fan.

In a Door, into a Fight, Out a Door, into a Chase: Moviemaking Remembered by the Guy at the Door. William Witney. McFarland, 1995. Hardcover, 256 pages.

Recently recognized as one of the great directors of the century, William Witney contributed extensively to the "B" western genre in his life time. Witney was largely responsible for the kinetic action method of directing, and his innovation is still an influence today. This book is full of movie memories as seen from the directorial chair. Recounting his work with Captain Marvel, the Lone Ranger, Roy Rogers, Gene Autry, Red Ryder, and others, this book leaves you wanting more — just the way Mr. Witney would have liked it.

Stunt Man: The Autobiography of Yakima Canutt. Oliver Drake and Yakima Canutt. Walker and Company, 1979. Hardcover, 252 pages.

Yakima Canutt and Harry Carey Sr. were the backbone of the stunt industry in the early Hollywood western years. In this book by Oliver Drake, one of the most prominent and influential serial directors, the story of Yakima Canutt is told for the first time. Great reading about a stunt pioneer. An added bonus in this book is the foreword by Charlton Heston and an epilogue by John Wayne.

COLLECTIVE BIOGRAPHIES

A Biographical Dictionary of Silent Film Western Actors and Actresses. George Katchmer. McFarland, 2002. Hardcover, 488 pages.

Mr. Katchmer has done a remarkable job in this dictionary of silent film stars. Each listing includes a detailed biography, western filmography and photograph. Large in its scope, the book rarely misses a beat. Katchmer has produced a milestone book for silent film fans everywhere.

Ladies of the Western. Michael G. Fitzgerald and Boyd Magers. McFarland, 2002. Hardcover, 336 pages.

A followup volume to *Westerns Women* (listed below) by Magers and Fitzgerald, this book features 51 interviews with the females stars of "A" and "B" westerns from the 1950s and 1960s. Complete with 150 photographs, this book is fascinating reading.

The Round-Up: A Pictorial History of Western and Television Stars Through the Years. Donald Keys, editor. Empire, 1995. Hardcover, 320 pages.

Donald Keys has compiled an excellent photo resource of more than 300 stars, sidekicks, villains, heroines and assorted players. Encompassing television and movie stars, this book is a great addition to any library.

Sweethearts of the Sage: Biographies and Filmographies of 258 Actresses Appearing in Western Movies. Buck Rainey. McFarland, 1992. Hardcover, 652 pages.

Buck Rainey has done a superlative job in this volume of his work. The short biographies and filmographies for each of the 258 ladies are both informative and accurate. Another recommended book for any library.

Westerns Women: Interviews with 50 Leading Ladies of Movie and Television Westerns from the 1930s to the 1960s. Boyd Magers and Michael G. Fitzgerald. McFarland, 1999. Hardcover, 288 pages.

Fifty leading ladies tell their stories to Magers and Fitzgerald. Great first-person information for the fan of early westerns.

Character Studies

The Films of the Cisco Kid. Francis Nevins Jr. Empire. Softcover, 100 pages.

This book examines the Cisco Kid in his various incarnations from the first film, to the radio show, to the fan favorite television series with Duncan Renaldo and Leo Carillo. This volume includes a filmography, 100 photographs and much more. No Cisco Kid fan should be without this book

The Films of Hopalong Cassidy. Francis Nevins Jr. World of Yesterday. Softcover, 100 pages.

An in-depth look at the screen life of Hopalong Cassidy, one of America's favorite western heroes. This book covers the Hopalong Cassidy movies and the long running TV series in detail. Rare photographs are included in this Hopalong Cassidy must-have.

From Out of the Past: A Pictorial History of the Lone Ranger. Dave Holland. Holland House 1988. Hardcover, 444 pages.

Absolutely the best Lone Ranger book available. Just as the Roy Rogers book by Robert Phillips encompasses all, this captures the story of the Lone Ranger from his creation at the desk of Fran Striker and his team to the most recent history (as of 1988). With chapters on radio, print, movies, television and merchandising, it leaves little unsaid. Stunning in its completeness, it is a necessity for any Lone Ranger fan.

The Lone Ranger Pictorial Scrapbook. Lee Felbinger. Countryside, 1986. Softcover, 260 pages.

From the rousing image of the Lone Ranger bursting from the front cover, straight through to the end of the book, Lee Felbinger (the world's foremost Lone Ranger collector) presents the most complete Ranger memorabilia collection in existence. Written after the Lone Ranger's fiftieth anniversary, it gives a thorough look at the Lone Ranger in merchandising.

Silent Hoofbeats. Bobby Copeland. Empire, 2001. Softcover, 136 pages.

Bobby Copeland's labor of love, *Silent Hoofbeats*, is a treasure. A complete listing and description of each rider and horse from our favorite western movies are included. Entertaining and informative anecdotes from riders, trainers, and co-workers accompany each entry. Truly a one-of-a-kind book.

Those Great Cowboy Sidekicks. David Rothel. Empire, 2001. Hardcover, 328 pages.

No "B" western was complete without a sidekick. David Rothel examines our favorite characters such as Andy Devine, Gabby Hayes, Al "Fuzzy" St. John, Smiley Burnette, Pat Buttram, Pat Brady, and others. He profiles

39 sidekicks through reminiscences from the actors themselves as well as those who knew these unforgettable characters. Relatives, directors, extras, their co-stars, and even the actual sidekicks contributed to this engaging book.

Western Gunslingers in Fact and on Film: Hollywood's Famous Lawmen and Outlaws. Buck Rainey. McFarland, 1997. Softcover, 349 pages.

Buck Rainey, in this book, tackles the difficult issue of historical accuracy. He compares the heroes and villains of the old west as seen by Hollywood to the facts and their real lives. This book is both entertaining and educational.

Who Was That Masked Man? The Story of the Lone Ranger. David Rothel. A. S. Barnes, 1976. Hardcover, 280 pages.

As one of the first authors to cover the history of the Masked Man, David Rothel had the unique opportunity to interview James Jewel, George Trendle, Clayton Moore and many others no longer with us who were actively involved with the onscreen and on-air Lone Ranger phenomenon. From this perspective, David Rothel is able to give us a first-person look at the evolution of the Lone Ranger and Tonto. From the early days of the radio show to the controversy surrounding *The Legend of the Lone Ranger*, David Rothel gives us a good overview of the legend the Lone Ranger has become.

Books About Westerns and the Entertainment Industry

RADIO

The Great Radio Heroes. Jim Harmon. McFarland, 2001. Softcover, 256 pages.

In 1967, Jim Harmon published the first edition of *The Great Radio Heroes*. Thirty-three years later, McFarland presented this expanded, corrected and illustrated edition for those who missed the first. The romance of the radio was real: Imaginations soared as rocket ships flew over the moon and between stars, and gunfights came to life in millions of young minds with nothing more than a good sound effects man backing up the fantasy. Jim Harmon provides production information and reminisces about your favorite dramas in this classic work.

Radio Mystery and Adventure and Its Apearances in Film, Television and Other Media. Jim Harmon. McFarland, 1992. Hardcover, 302 pages.

Radio was king from the 1920s through to the 1950s. Mystery and adventure were two of the primary themes common to this era's productions.

Jim Harmon, radio historian and producer, has listed each drama with genre, cast, broadcast dates, air dates, sponsors, networks, and production credits, and includes a critical essay. If the series crossed over to other media, the secondary appearances are also included. Perfect for the radio drama fan.

Raised on Radio: In Quest of the Lone Ranger, Jack Benny, Amos 'n' Andy, the Shadow, Mary Noble, the Great Gildersleeve, Fibber McGee and Molly ... and Other Lost Heroes from Radio's Heyday. Gerald Nachman. University of California Press, 2000. Softcover, 535 pages.

During its heyday, radio was incomparable. The scope of radio drama reached from comedy, to romance, to science fiction, to westerns, to crime and detective stories, to "hero" series. This book is an excellent overview of the whole genre. It dares to compare contemporary entertainment to our radio roots, and through these comparisons the reader who was not raised on radio can understand the impact the radio era had on its listeners. For radio drama history, this book is highly recommended.

The Western Logs. Terry Salomonson. Self published, 1998. Coil bound, 130 pages.

Terry Salomonson has done a remarkable job in the creation of his radio log series. In his *Western Logs*, he has compiled a brief history of 44 major western radio series. Included with each entry is a cast and production listing, sponsor history, and air time and dates, with episode titles where available. *Roy Rogers, Gene Autry, Tom Mix, Hopalong Cassidy, Lassie, Tales of the Texas Rangers, Gunsmoke, The Cisco Kid*, and many more favorite shows are found in this guide. For the radio fan, this source is indispensable. Due to the show's longevity, *The Lone Ranger* is missing from this guide, but his history is discussed in Salomonson's *The Lone Ranger Log* (110 pages).

Wyxie Wonderland. Dick Osgood. Popular Press, 1981. Hardcover.

WXYZ was a magical place to be. Through the words of Dick Osgood, we can be there too. In *Wyxie Wonderland*, Osgood offers a diary of the early years of radio drama's most enduring studio. The Lone Ranger, Sgt. Preston, The Green Hornet and many other classic characters were born in these fertile offices. Osgood gives us his impressions, shares his stories, and offers insight into a place where "once upon a time" was really true.

STUDIOS

Universal-International Westerns, 1947–1963. Gene Blottner. McFarland, 2000. Hardcover, 368 pages.

As a major player in the western production field, Universal-International gave us many memorable films. A complete filmography is included as well as over 120 photographs, a bibliography, and insights into each film. Interviews are seamlessly interwoven into the entries and add to the book's overall presentation. Highly recommended.

The Vanishing Legion: A History of Mascot Pictures, 1927–1935. Jon Tuska. McFarland, 1982 (hardcover) and 1999 (softcover), 224 pages.

Mascot Pictures, in its nine-year history, gave us Gene Autry, Tom Mix, John Wayne, Rin Tin Tin, and other lesser known stars. This beautifully written book pays tribute to the contribution of this early production company to the movie serial industry. Based on thorough research and personal interviews, *The Vanishing Legion* gives us a critical look at all Mascot productions. An informative appendix includes cast lists, technical credits, chapter titles, and rare advertisements and stills.

MUSIC

It Was Always the Music. Eric Van Hamersveld. R & R, 2003. Hardcover, 400 pages.

Eric Van Hamersveld has produced a landmark with this book, the result of six years of dedicated research on Roy Rogers' music. The book itself, at 400 pages, is packed full of photographs from 28 movies, song sheets, film credits, story synopses and notes on why each song was included in the movie. An optional 3 CD set (with 160 songs) is also available as a companion piece. A truly stunning collection and book for any Roy Rogers fan!

Mystery of the Masked Man's Music: A Search for the Music Used on the Lone Ranger. Reginald M. Jones. Scarecrow, 2002. Hardcover.

The second most asked question in the Lone Ranger series (right after "Who was that masked man?") is "Where is that music from?" Reginald Jones answers that question in this fascinating story. This book answers the questions, "Who recorded it?" "When?" "Where?" and "Where did it come from?" Jumping from New York, to Detroit, to Mexico City, and back to Hollywood, this story offers more than meets the ear.

Singing in the Saddle: The History of the Singing Cowboy. Douglas B. Green. Vanderbilt University Press, 2002. Hardcover, 268 pages.

Doug Green, noted historian, tackles the broad topic of the singing cowboy and thoroughly succeeds. From Billy Hill to the Sons of the Pioneers, he handles each topic and star well and in depth. Truly a book worthy of any western movie fan's library.

MOVIE SERIALS AND CLIFFHANGERS

In the Nick of Time. William C. Cline. McFarland, 1984 (hardcover) and 1997 (softcover), 293 pages.

The importance of the serial industry is discussed in this fifteen-chapter book. The value of the cliffhangers cannot be overestimated as a training ground for both actors and technical staff. From the first serial, *The Indians Are Coming*, to the last, the story is told in an enlightening style that begs you to read on. The appendix includes all sound serials released from 1930 to 1956, complete with titles, release dates and companies, production company directors and cast members.

The Republic Chapterplays: A Complete Filmography of the Serials Released by Republic Pictures Corporation, 1934–1955. R. M. Hayes. McFarland, 1992 (hardcover) and 2000 (softcover), 176 pages.

Chances are if you went to see a movie serial during the 1930s, 1940s or 1950s, it was a Republic production. The Republic eagle, during a twenty year period, was the "good movie making seal of approval" for millions of fans. This book features an insightful and concise introduction and history of Republic, its rise and fall. The book lists all Republic serials in order of production, offering production credits, release and re-release dates, sequels, and running times. This book is a perfect companion when you turn on Captain Marvel, Zorro, Jungle Girl, the G Men, or Commander Cody.

Republic Confidential Volume 1: The Studio. Jack Mathis. Mathis Advertising, 1989. Hardcover, 512 pages.

In this sequel to *Valley of the Cliffhangers*, Jack Mathis satisfies even the most critical Republic Picture fan with hundreds of photos and illustrations.

Republic Confidential Volume 2: The Players. Jack Mathis. Mathis Advertising, 1992. Hardcover, 270 pages.

Excellent in-depth coverage of the Republic players. Presented in two sections (contractees and a super index), this reference book gives you everything you ever wanted to know about the Republic stars (and some lesser lights), from contracts to their smallest appearances. A jewel for the movie fan.

Serials-ly Speaking: Essays on Cliffhangers. William C. Cline (Foreword by Frank Coghlan Jr.). McFarland, 1994 (hardcover) and 2000 (softcover), 271 pages.

William C. Cline was an outstanding columnist for *Big Reel*, a monthly periodical for fans of old movies. In this collection of essays, he focuses on the fans of the serial: what they saw in the serials as children, what they see in them today, and why they still enjoy them. A brief commentary preceding each essay puts the piece into context and explains why Cline wrote it. A great way to relive your misspent youth.

To Be Continued. Ken Weiss. Bonanza, 1972. Hardcover, 343 pages.

The first complete listing of the 230 movie serials produced in Hollywood from 1929 to 1956. The listings are arranged in chronological order, and in each section in order of release. Each serial description includes main characters, number of chapters, writer and director, studio, and a brief synopsis of the film. Rare photographs are included. Who was the "King of the Serials"? This book can answer your questions. A must-have for the serial fan.

Valley of the Cliffhangers. Jack Mathis. Mathis Advertising, 1975. Hardcover.

Jack Mathis has written one incredible book. Copious in its detail, this book includes all 66 Republic serials produced between 1934 and 1955. The result is an encyclopedic mass of information. With this book, you can even identify the backup players! As one of the first reference books on movie serials, this one gets real expensive and is worth every penny.

Valley of the Cliffhangers Supplement. Jack Mathis. Mathis Advertising, 1995. Hardcover, 512 pages.

A truly incredible book detailing each of the 849 chapters (from the 66 movie serials) produced by Republic Pictures from 1934 to 1955. Each serial is broken down into a chapter-by-chapter synopsis, and the performers are listed as well. Rare posters and color photos are included to enhance your reading pleasure. Designed to be used with the *Valley of the Cliffhangers*, this book helps us make sense of the often-twisted plots of the mighty serials of our youth.

LOCATIONS AND MOVIE RANCHES

An Ambush of Ghosts. David Rothel. Empire. Hardcover, 304 pages.

David Rothel, in this profusely illustrated (over 350 photos) hardcover edition, takes us back to the locations where Randolph Scott, the Lone Ranger, Roy Rogers, Tex Ritter, John Wayne, and many more stars rode, fought and died. The photos compare what the area was then with what it is now. A compelling book written by a great contemporary author.

Quiet on the Set! Motion Picture History at the Iverson Movie Ranch. Robert G. Sherman. Sherway. Softcover.

Once the premier western movie location ranch, Iverson was the home to over 2,000 films over a period of 70 years. Robert Sherman has compiled an extensive history of this important movie location complete with rare photographs. If you enjoyed the B westerns as a youth, this book will entertain you and bring back many memories.

EPISODE GUIDES, CAST LISTINGS, FILM LISTINGS

The BFI Companion to the Western. Edward Buscombe. Atheneum, 1988. Hardcover, 432 pages.

The BFI Companion to the Western is a great resource for the American fan. Written from a British point of view, it is divided into sections on history, movies, movie stars, and TV shows. The text is supplemented by both black and white and color photos and includes a great bibliography.

Gunsmoke. SuZanne and Gabor Barabas. McFarland, 1990. Hardcover, 848 pages.

As the longest running prime time series in history, *Gunsmoke* (1955–1975) shaped the mindset of the viewing public as it related to justice in the American west and was influenced by the culture of the time. This book offers a complete history and analysis of the *Gunsmoke* radio and television series. It is a vital book for *Gunsmoke* fans of any age. Photographs, interviews, episode guides, appendix, and a thoroughly detailed bibliography are included.

The Official TV Western Round Up Book. Neil Summers and Roger M. Crowley. Hardcover, 208 pages.

Neil Summers, veteran stuntman, and Roger Crowley have compiled interviews with Will Hutchins, Kelo Henderson, Whitey Hughes, Gail Davis, John Hart, Rand Brooks, and many more in this intriguing collection. Great for the connoisseur of western trivia and television culture. Neil Summers helps us remember the work of our youth and wish we were there again.

The Shoot-em-ups Ride Again. Buck Rainey. World of Yesterday. Softcover, 315 pages.

Covering western movie history from 1928 to 1978, Buck Rainey includes 1600 movies and telefilms in this extensive treatment of the western genre. Including western television show reviews from 1948 onward and more than 150 photographs, this book is a great resource.

Television Western Players of the Fifties: A Biographical Encyclopedia of All Regular Cast Members in Western Series, 1949–1959. Everett Aaker. McFarland, 1997. Hardcover, 588 pages.

For ten years, westerns ruled the television range. The Lone Ranger was the first to appear on the small screen, and thirty-two western series followed in prime-time slots by 1959. This volume includes biographical information, opinions of contemporaries, and information on the "big break" for each actor and actress from the many westerns (more than 80) produced during the 1950s. This well researched and written book is invaluable for the TV western fan.

Television Westerns Episode Guide: All United States Series, 1949–1996. Harris Lentz III. McFarland, 1997. Hardcover, 576 pages.

Similar in presentation to Lentz's *Western and Frontier Film and Television Credits,* this book lists cast and production personnel, episode air dates, and much more information.

Western and Frontier Film and Television Credits, 1903–1995. Harris Lentz III. McFarland, 1996. Hardcover, 1796 pages in 2 volumes.

An intensive and comprehensive listing of television and movie credits for all productions from the earliest known film. Including a section on actors and actresses, a section on directors and production personnel, and an alphabetical film listing, this book also covers the television years, with listings including series title, air dates, cast and all credits. One of the great resources for the videophile.

Western Movies: A TV and Video Guide to 4200 Genre Films. Michael R. Pitts, compiler. McFarland, 1986 (hardcover) and 1997 (softcover), 635 pages.

Impressive in its scope, this guide lists over 4200 western films produced in Hollywood. Each entry lists title, releasing company, year of release, running time, and indication of whether the film is in color or black and white, cast listing, plot synopsis, and a brief critical review. An incredibly useful reference book for the western videophile.

White Hats and Silver Spurs: Interviews with 24 Stars of Film and Television Westerns of the Thirties Through the Sixties. Herb Fagen. McFarland, 1996. Hardcover, 253 pages.

For over 40 years, westerns ruled the movie theatres and the small screen. Herb Fagen has interviewed 24 of the most influential surviving actors of the era. Ben Johnson, Lois Hall, Sue Anne Langdon, Lee Aaker, John Agar, Clint Walker and others give their unique insight into the productions and personalities that made westerns so popular.

Miscellaneous Topics

B-Western Boot Hill. Bobby Copeland. Empire, 2002. Softcover, 216 pages.

Bobby Copeland, in the course of his research for his books, has amassed an amazing collection of information. Over ten years, his collection of B Western obituaries and articles has resulted in this timeless reference book. Complete with birth and death dates, real names of the popular western stars and sidekicks, places of burial, and reprints of actual obituaries from local papers, this book is destined to be a classic.

The Lone Ranger's Code of the West. Jim Lichtman, Mark Palmer, Fran Striker Jr. Scribblers Ink, 1996. Softcover, 261 pages.

Who better to teach a moral lesson to contemporary society than the Lone Ranger? Jim Lichtman retells eight classic Lone Ranger tales and relates each story to one ethical mindset through a series of conversations. The Lone Ranger and Jim Lichtman converse and discuss the implications of each behavior. In so doing, they illustrate a series of moral lessons so needed in our difficult times.

They Went Thataway. James Horowitz. Ballantine, 1976. Softcover, 280 pages.

An affectionate look at the mighty "B" movie, its birth and demise. Covering the history of the "B" movies, and including some of the last interviews with some of the greats of the west, this leaves you wanting to read more. Included are interviews with Tim McCoy, Rex Allen, Charles Starrett, Duncan Renaldo, Joel McCrea, Russell Hayden, Sunset Carson, Gene Autry, and Jimmy Wakely.

Trail Talk. Bobby Copeland. Empire, 1999. Softcover, 168 pages.

From the more than 40 conventions Bobby Copeland has attended, he has compiled an absorbing collection of quotes and comments from the stars of our youth. Try and put this one down; bet you can't!

Price Guides and Collectibles Guides

Toys

The Encyclopedia of Marx Action Figures. Tom Heaton. Krause, 1999. Softcover, 176 pages.

The world of Marx toys comes alive with this excellent Marx action figure encyclopedia. Containing information on the more than 230 figures produced, pictures of the boxes, notes on accessories, and three pricing levels, this reference work is perfect for the Marx-ologist!

Hopalong Cassidy Collectibles. Joseph J. Caro. Cowboy Collector, 1997. Softcover, 284 pages.

This incredible book by Joseph Caro, the leading Hoppy authority in the United States, contains over 1200 color photographs of rare to common Hopalong memorabilia from the 1930s to the present. Listed with each photo along with a description are market values and conditions. Authorized by U. S. Television (Sagebrush Entertainment), this book is a necessity for all Hoppy collectors worldwide.

O'Brien's Collecting Toys. Elizabeth Stephan, editor. Krause, 1999. Softcover, 700 pages.

While not exclusively a western collectibles price guide, this book offers a great overview of the many toys you can find. Zorro, the Lone

Ranger, Roy Rogers, Hopalong Cassidy, and a variety of other western toys can be found in this giant 700 page book.

Official Hake's Price Guide to Character Toys. Ted Hake. House of Collectibles, 2002. Softcover, 856 pages.

Ted Hake, North America's foremost collectible toy expert, has produced this excellent, comprehensive price guide for over 360 product categories. Complete with over 10,000 photographs and 30,000 prices, this definitive work is a must-have.

Roy Rogers and Dale Evans Toys and Memorabilia: Identification and Values. P. Allan Coyle. Collector Books, 2000. Softcover, 240 pages.

Similar in scope and presentation to *The Ultimate Roy Rogers Collection* by Ron Lenius, this volume presents 700 full-color photos of Roy Rogers and Dale Evans story books, lunch boxes, school supplies, albums, records, movie posters, watches, cereal premiums, guns and holsters, and more. Individual pricing is included with every photo.

The Roy Rogers Book: A Reference and Trivia Scrapbook. David Rothel. Empire, 1987. Softcover, 224 pages.

David Rothel has done an excellent job of combining a reference book, scrapbook, and trivia handbook on the "King of the Cowboys." Containing almost 200 photos and many hard-to-find facts, it serves as a great guide for the Rogers collector.

Television's Cowboys, Gunfighters, and Their Cap Pistols. Rudy D'Angelo. Antique Trader, 1999. Softcover, 196 pages.

Rudy D'Angelo has compiled an impressive labor of love. In this comprehensive history and survey of the collectible cap pistol, he presents a history of each manufacturer and each character represented by the pistol set. Profusely illustrated with over 200 photographs, this book also includes a well respected price guide. Highly recommended for the toy gun collector.

The Ultimate Roy Rogers Collection: Identification and Price Guide. Ron Lenius. Krause, 2001. Softcover, 208 pages.

The most comprehensive listing of Roy Rogers, Dale Evans, Gabby Hayes, Bullet and Trigger collectibles ever compiled. This truly is the ultimate reference for all Roy Rogers collectors. The book contains over 1000 full-color photographs of rare and vintage collectibles, along with individual pricing for each item. As a bonus, an interview with Dusty Rogers is included. The best guide ever published.

COMIC BOOKS, COMIC ART AND BOOKS

Big Little Books: A Collectors' Reference and Value Guide. Larry Jacobs. Collectors Books, 1996. Softcover, 175 pages.

Larry Jacobs has compiled an excellent source of information on the collecting and valuation of Big Little Books and the variations thereof. Over 800 items are listed with photographs and value ranges for each. An indispensable book for the kid at heart.

Collectible Magazines. Henkel. HarperCollins, 2001. Softcover.

As with hardcover books, the field of magazine collecting has undergone a transformation. Covering all genres and generations of magazines, this guide serves as a comprehensive source for pricing, grading, and market conditions, and presents information necessary for the collector at large.

Comic Art Price Guide. Jerry Weist. Acturian, 2000. Softcover, 560 pages.

The field of original comic book, pulp magazine, and newspaper strip art has undergone a transformation in the past decade. Once considered of little value, original artwork is now considered an investment. Jerry Weist has compiled an impressive list of values, artists, and formats for the seasoned and beginning collector. A market review, a hobby primer, and, of course, the price guide combine to make this guide a real winner.

Hancer's Price Guide to Paperback Books. Kevin Hancer. Wallace-Homestead (Chilton), 1990. Softcover, 355 pages.

An indispensable resource for the book collector. Containing information on paperbacks from 1939 to 1959, it lists publishers alphabetically, along with book number, title, author, price range, and genre. Authors are indexed, with publisher and book number. Hard to find, but worth it for the fan of western literature.

Official Price Guide to Collecting Books. Marie Tedford and Pat Goudey. House of Collectibles, 2001. Softcover, 482 pages.

As the market for antiquarian books grows, so does the need for solid contemporary information. Marie Tedford and Pat Goudey present hardcover pricing and history from the early 1800s to the late twentieth century with authority. The covered material includes the "classics," the rare editions, and popular contemporary authors.

Overstreet Comic Book Price Guide. Robert M. Overstreet. Avon/Gemstone, annually. Softcover.

The bible for comic book collectors, this annual publication compiled by Robert Overstreet is a must-have. Listing all known comic books printed since 1842, this monster guide lists each title alphabetically, with publishing information, run dates, art and writing credits where possible, and values for four conditions. Informative articles, a market analysis, and "top 50" lists all make this series invaluable.

Whitman Juvenile Books: Reference and Value Guide. David Brown and Virginia Brown. Collectors Books, 1999. Softcover, 143 pages.

What a great reference book for the young at heart! Containing more than 400 large, sharp, full-color photographs of the Whitman hardcovers, this book lists values and descriptions, and includes information on the background of the Whitman editions and company.

Radio and TV Memorabilia

The Official Price Guide to Radio TV and Movie Memorabilia. Thomas E Hudgeons III, editor. House of Collectibles, 1986. Softcover, 528 pages.

A vital source for pricing, product descriptions, and general hobby information. Containing information and pricing on animation cells, autographs, costumes, movie sheet music, movie poster and lobby cards, radio premiums, *TV Guide* issues, and a general TV memorabilia section, this book serves as a primer for those just getting into collecting.

Radio and TV Premiums: A Guide to the History and Value of Radio and TV Premiums. Jim Harmon. Krause, 1988. Softcover, 288 pages.

Jim Harmon, in his research on radio history, has built up an amazing knowledge base. In this book, he lists alphabetically the character and the premiums; then he cross-references each list to the other. The result is an easy-to-use book for collectors of premiums everywhere. Comic books are also covered. Photographs, price ranges, and a history of the premiums are included in this invaluable book.

Records

A Music Lover's Guide to Record Collecting. Dave Thompson. Backbeat, 2002. Softcover, 320 pages.

Dave Thompson has written a lively book. Delving into every topic concerning recording collecting from 78s to MPs, he offers engaging essays that educate the buyer and collector of records and discs. An excellent introduction to this growing hobby.

The Official Price Guide to Records 2001. Jerry Osborne. House of Collectibles, annually. Softcover, 864 pages.

More than 100,000 prices are listed in recent editions of this essential price guide for the record collector. Listing every charted hit from 1926, this book is organized by artist and group for easy access. New editions are published frequently. This is a perfect companion for *A Music Lovers Guide* by Dave Thompson.

The Books of Allan G. Barbour

Allan G. Barbour was an incredible man, and one to whom we lovers of movie serials, "B" westerns, or anything Republic owe an eternal debt. It was through his efforts that the archival material from Republic was preserved and pushed back into the public eye.

Through his research skills, interviews with Republic legends, and sheer love of the medium and art form known as the cliffhanger, he wrote and published the first serious treatise on serials, *The Serials of Republic*, in 1965. He followed that up with *Cliffhanger, Days of Thrills and Adventures, Screen Nostalgia*, and *Movie Ads of the Past*. He passed away in February 2002, after contributing to film festivals and pursuing serious film research for 37 years. He led the charge, and he will always be remembered.

I have not included his books in the listings above. I cannot find copies. I know, however, that they belong in the list. If you are lucky enough to find or already own copies of these gems, consider yourself truly fortunate: You are holding history.

Publisher Contact Information

Bruce Hershenson Publishing
PO Box 874
West Plains MO 65775
417-256-9616
www.brucehershenson.com

Countryside Advertising
Box 159
Badman Rd
Green Lane PA 18054

Earl Blair Enterprises
PO Box 87
Toney AL 35773

Empire Publishing, Inc.
PO Box 717
Madison NC 27025-0717
336-427-5850
www.empirepublishinginc.com
movietv@pop.vnet.net

Holland House
760 Chief Thundercloud Ln
Lone Pine CA 93345
619-876-4725

Krause Publications
700 E State St
Iola WI 54900-0001
www.krause.com

Lawrence Hopper
50 S First St 8A
Bergenfield, NJ 07621-2453
PHL2@Juno.com

Mario De Marco
152 Maple St
W Boylston MA 01583
508-835-4085

McFarland & Company, Inc.,
Publishers
Box 611
Jefferson NC 28640
336-246-4460
www.mcfarlandpub.com

R & R Publications
www.royrogersmusic.com

Scarecrow Press, Inc.
4501 Forbes Blvd
Ste 200
Lanham MD 20706
800-462-6420
www.scarecrowpress.com

Scribblers Ink
www.scribblers-ink.com

Taylor Publishing Company
1550 West Mockingbird Ln
Dallas TX 75235

Terry Salomonson
PO Box 347
Howell MI 48844-0347
terryotr@ismi.net

World of Yesterday Publishing
(BearManor Media)
PO Box 750
Boalsburg PA 16827
www.bersmanormedia.bizland.com

Wyatt Classics, Inc.
1012 Vance St
Raleigh NC 27608

6

Trail Gear: Collectibles

As long as there have been cowboy heroes, there have been collectibles. The TV and movie cowboys of the 1920s, 1930s, 1940s and up to the late 1970s when *Gunsmoke* went off the air were celebrated with an assortment of associated memorabilia ranging from books to yo-yos.

The advent of talkies in the late 1920s brought a new approach to the marketing of movie heroes, beginning with the production of "nickel cards" featuring Tom Mix, Tim McCoy, Buck Jones, Harry Carey, or Fredd Scott.

Movie serials, produced by the Gower Gulch Gang, filled the screens and children filled the seats. Gene Autry, Tom Mix, John Wayne, and the silent stars who successfully made the transition starred week after week in "dusters" and the chapter plays.

Meanwhile, radio drama, comedy and serials, broadcast into the night around North America, introduced *The Lone Ranger, The Green Hornet, Gunsmoke, Death Valley Days,* and *Sergeant Preston* to the audiences.

Comic strips, which had made their debut in the 1900s, assumed their now-classic form during the 1930s. Numerous adventure heroes first appeared on newspaper pages. Characters from the radio jumped onto the comic pages, and then later into comic books.

As successful promotional campaigns for the Lone Ranger, Tom Mix, and Hopalong Cassidy opened eyes all around North America, character-related memorabilia began to appear in stores.

Popular actors and their characters began to appear in Big Little Books, comic books, character-related novels, games, toothbrushes, pistol sets, secret decoders, character costumes, and hundreds of other products licensed by copyright holders.

Many characters also hit the big screen as the movie serial art form was being developed by the many studios. The Lone Ranger, the Green Hornet, Gene Autry, Buffalo Bill, Annie Oakley, and Jesse James starred in multi-chaptered adventures. The "B" western was born in Poverty Row in Hollywood, filmed in Lone Pine, and lived in the imaginations of the children who spent Saturdays watching their heroes gallop across the screen.

Stars like Roy Rogers, Gabby Hayes, Monte Hale, Rex Allen, Clayton Moore, Jay Silverheels, Gene Autry, Tom Tyler, Tom Steele, and others too numerous to mention criss-crossed the continent in thousands of roles in thousands of movies for over 25 years.

The production of cowboy collectibles hit its stride in the 1940s and 1950s, when the kings of marketing (Gene Autry, Roy Rogers, Hopalong Cassidy, and the Lone Ranger) dominated the marketplace.

The Big Four branched out into television, radio, clothing, books, comics, western themed toys, trading cards, music, and lunch kits and pushed the frontiers of character marketing. Today, there are over 350 recognized categories of collectibles, and the Big Four are represented in all of them.

Almost 5,000 licensed Roy Rogers and Hopalong Cassidy products were marketed in one year! Hopalong Cassidy reportedly earned $25 million from collectibles in 1951 alone. He and Roy Rogers were more fortunate than Gene Autry, who did not own his own rights until the early 1950s. Later, when Gene Autry formed Flying A Productions to produce his own shows, he began to get a bigger piece of the merchandising pie.

Like all successful marketing campaigns, promotions for the Big Four went through phases, recruiting five types of food sponsors—cereal, bread, candy, milk and beverages— as well as producers of clothing, play-sets, books, school supplies, marbles, knives and numerous other products.

Today the books, puzzles, pistols, clothes, cars, banks, radio premiums, marbles, western town sets, and figurines that we played with as children are the collectibles that we seek.

Posters and Other Art

COMMEMORATIVE ARTWORK AND POSTERS

Relatively recently, the field of western collectibles has been blessed with the addition of commemorative artwork. Fueled by the revivals of the early westerns and western stars and the birth and growth of the convention movement, artists have sought to celebrate their heroes in their artwork.

Many of the cowboy legend museums carry prints of such tributes, while others have long since disappeared into private collections. Occasionally surfacing on eBay, at collectible auctions, or on estate dispersal sales, these items are truly unique and well worth the investment.

Stars pictured in tributes include the Lone Ranger, Roy Rogers, Dale

Opposite: Gabby Hayes tribute poster. (Courtesy Roy Rogers–Dale Evans Museum)

2002 Hopalong Cassidy commemorative poster by Tom Yeates. (Courtesy Ground Zero)

Evans, Gabby Hayes, John Wayne, Jimmy Stewart, Tonto, Tom Mix, and many, many more heroes of the silver screen.

There are always commemorative posters being produced. They are advertised for sale at festivals, auctions, and on eBay. A terrific commemorative poster of Hopalong Cassidy is currently available from Ground Zero at:

> Ground Zero LLC
> 625 Colony Rd
> Clifton CO 81520
> 970-523-3575
> www.comicsspotlight.com

The value of commemorative posters varies. Keep your eyes sharp, saddle partner: Treasure is always on the horizon somewhere.

POSTERS, PRODUCTION STILLS, AND LOBBY CARDS

Posters, stills, and lobby cards are increasingly collectible. Due to the recent dispersion of major private and studio collections and the influence of the Internet, the hobby is growing by leaps and bounds.

"Posters" is a general term to describe various sizes and styles of promotional materials. You can buy one-sheet (27" × 41"), two-sheet (30" × 40"), three-sheet (41" × 81"), six-sheet (82" × 81") and reproduction posters. Lobby cards come in either mini (8½" × 11") or regular (11" × 14"). Stills come in regular (8½" × 11") or poster size (11" × 14"), and inserts are 14" × 36".

The styles of posters have changed since their introduction in France in 1895. Hand painted posters were common during the 1920s and 1930s. Stone lithography printing led to offset lithography, even though color richness was diminished to increase image clarity.

Each studio had its own style of posters. RKO, Metro-Goldwyn-Mayer, Paramount, Warner Bros., and 20th Century–Fox each emphasized different design elements. RKO utilized watercolors and pastels, while MGM used bold primary colors. Paramount's posters were lettered more boldly (similar to MGM's). The posters of 20th Century–Fox were the most artistic, and those of Warner Bros. were perhaps the least so.

The National Screen Service took over poster distribution from 1942 to 1948. The NSS introduced a two-part coding system that is extensively used by collectors today.

From 1937 to 1960, almost 200 million posters were produced in America. Most of these were destroyed or thrown away as soon as the movie finished its run. Today, these posters are difficult to find and ever more rare in flat unfolded condition.

Lobby cards, once an anticipated part of every movie, went into decline in the 1970s as studios put less money into theater-based promotions and poured more into television. Nevertheless, they remain an integral part of a movie collector's portfolio. Originally issued in numbered sets of eight, they included a title card and selected scenes from the movie. Quite often, they featured a smaller version of the poster artwork or scenes from the movie.

Complete sets are the most desirable but, of course, the most difficult to find. Individual cards remain the most easily found and reasonably priced.

Movie, television, and production stills are readily available. With the advent of digital technologies, accurate reproductions of original stills are more common. Stills generally come in three sizes: miniatures (5" × 7"), regular (8" × 10"), and lobby size (11" × 14").

With prices starting in the $2 range for black and white, and color around $5, a stills collection is the least expensive movie image collection to start. Major stills retailers maintain an Internet presence and all sell on eBay, making this hobby more accessible — and at the same time, more overwhelming.

Jimmy Wakely *Range Renegades* lobby card, 1950.

Authenticity is a major issue in collecting stills. With digital scanning and printing so prevalent today, how can we tell if the print we have is real or a reproduction? And does it matter?

If you as a collector knowingly purchased a reproduction still, then it doesn't matter at all. If you purchased a still thinking it was real, only to realize it is a reproduction, then the difficulty begins.

How can we tell the difference between a digitally reproduced image and a real photograph? There are a few clues we can go on.

First, if the still is supposed to be 40 years old, the paper will likely show signs of age in its color, smell, and feel. Some yellowing could be present; there could be a little stale smell; and the paper may be somewhat brittle. Chemically speaking, if the paper is not acid free, the pH could also be a clue.

Second, if the still came from a studio, it may be stamped on the back accordingly ("Property of...").

Opposite: The Phantom of the West **poster, 1931. (Courtesy Bruce Hershenson–Allen Archives)**

The source of the still may be a clue. If it comes from an unrecognized dealer, it may not be authentic. If you want only original posters or stills, you should look for dealers that carry only these items and not reproductions.

The price is also an indicator. Generally speaking, the more expensive a still from a recognized dealer, the more likely it is to be original.

The presence of autographs is a good indicator of the authenticity of the item. If you have a *Casablanca* still that Humphrey Bogart signed, it is probably not authentic since he died in the 1950s. The presence of a signature is not proof positive that the item is original. Many stars willingly sign reproduction photos for fans, even decades after the fact.

Pricing information can be found in the *Official Price Guide to Radio TV and Movie Memorabilia*, *The Almanac of Movie Poster Prices*, Jon Warren's *Movie Poster Prices*, and any of the Bruce Hershenson books available online at www.brucehershenson.com. Hershenson's postal and phone contact information is

> Bruce Hershenson
> PO Box 874
> West Plains MO 65775
> 417-256-9616

Jon Warren can be contacted at:

> Jon Warren
> 2401 Broad St
> Chattanooga TN 37408
> 423-265-5515
> www.jonwarren.com

Jon Warren has written several price guides on comic books and paperbacks, and his *Movie Poster Price Guide* is now in its fifth edition. He is a source to be trusted.

Heritage Auctions, primarily known for their amazing comic auctions, also are well respected dealers in movie posters, lobby cards, and stills. They can be found online at: www.heritagecomics.com, or by post or phone at

> 100 Highland Park Village
> Second Floor
> Dallas TX 75205
> 800-872-6467

Other dealers include:

Empire Publishing, Inc
PO Box 717
Madison NC 27025-0717
336-427-5850
movietv@vpop.net
(photos only)

The Movie Goods Store
6601 Center Dr W
Ste 500
Los Angeles CA 90045
310-342-8295
www.moviegoods.com
(includes online poster price guide)

The Movie Market
PO Box 699

San Juan Capistrano CA 92693
949-488-8444
www.moviemarket.com

Jerry Ohlinger's
Movie Materials Store
242 W 14th St
New York NY 10011
212-989-0869
www.moviematerials.com

www.cowboylegends.com
(photographs, lobby cards, music,
videos)

www.doamoviememorablia.com
(lobbies, posters, and more)

Autographs

The collecting of autographs is an exciting hobby. Autographs come in all shapes and sizes. They can be obtained in person (the most enjoy-able and exciting method) or through the mail, or purchased from recognized dealers. Pictures, novels, lobby cards, posters, business cards, trading cards, video jackets and programs can be signed. Your only limit is what the star is willing to sign, and what UPS will deliver.

Personal-encounter auto-graphs are the most satisfying. Sitting across from your favorite star and chatting is a priceless experience. Add the fact that the photo, book or program is signed just for you, and you can't lose. Autographs signed in person are the best assurance that the signature really is authentic.

Autograph hunters flock to Los Angeles every year for the

Picture with John Hart autograph.

Duncan Renaldo "Cisco Kid" photo printed from an autographed negative.

Celebrity Fan Show. Over the years, thousands of actors have patiently signed autographs for fans from all over North America. Soap opera fans can cruise with their idols and also see them in Florida at the Fan Fest. For western fans, the Golden Boot Awards held in Los Angeles hold a particular attraction as western entertainment professionals gather to honor their best.

Autographs can be requested via mail. Writing a polite, respectful letter to your favorite celebrity will usually bring some sort of signed item. The risk you take in asking (nicely) for an autograph is the question, again, of authenticity. Certificates of Authenticity (COA) can be obtained for some signatures and are issued by dealers, or in some cases by the person who obtained the item.

Dealers will often sell only authentic autographs obtained from reliable sources. As the market grows, signed items have more value than nonsigned ones, and as a result, fraudulent sellers prey on the less than wise. Purchased signed items are often accompanied by COAs. Many galleries do incredible work in matting and framing signed pictures.

As an autograph collector for several years, I have found some basic guidelines for collectors.

Not all addresses for stars are accurate. Some lists may be outdated, or the star may not reply to mail at that address. Autograph collecting magazines include information on authorized fan clubs and up-to-date address lists.

Be open to what they offer. Roy Rogers in his later life stopped signing autographs. Instead, he posed for pictures with his fans. Thousands of fans have as the centerpiece of their collection a precious picture with Roy or Dale or with Clayton Moore.

Be polite. Rude, boorish, and disrespectful letters do not receive replies.

Be respectful of the entertainer's time. Signing pictures is time consuming and exhausting work. Some stars now sell their autographed pictures for upwards of $20 in order to be compensated for their time.

Be considerate. If you mail items for signing, include a suitable amount for return postage. Best of all is a self-addressed mailer with postage affixed. That way, the star can simply sign the item, insert it in the mailer, and drop it in the mail.

Be patient. Neither UPS nor stars work on a deadline. Some stars take up to six months to return a letter, while some sign almost immediately. Remember, you are asking them to take a little out of their day to accommodate you, a total stranger, and your request for an autograph.

Be informed. Joining the Universal Autograph Collectors Club will educate you on the risks and rewards of this fascinating hobby. Be on

Autographed copy of *Monte Hale Western* comic.

the lookout for autograph magazines and books. You can always learn from professional collectors.

Be wary. Not all autographs are signed by the stars. Can you imagine receiving 200 (or 50,000) letters a week asking for your signature? Many popular stars employ secretaries to sign on their behalf, or use an Autopen. The Autopen signs the same on each picture. Such "signatures" can be recognized by comparing them to a certified one. Some "genuine" autographed photos are actually printed from an autographed negative. It's the star's signature, all right, but the fact is that it can be reproduced thousands of times simply by reprinting the negative.

Be appreciative. Remember, the star took time out of his or her day to sign your picture. Not all of your requests for autographs will bear fruit. Be thankful when they do.

Be legible. There is nothing worse than getting a letter from the star saying that he or she could not read your writing. Type your letter if you have to, or write neatly. Illegible letters will probably not generate a response.

The value of an autograph depends on several factors. First of all, the context of the signature will influence the value of the item. Personal letters, personal signed items, signed sympathy cards, personal checks, and contracts all have more value than a signed picture. The uniqueness of a signed item can increase the value. The death of an actor can cause the existing signatures to increase in value. The frequency of verifiable signatures will partly determine the value: low supply equals high price, and vice versa.

The timing of autograph requests can affect your response time. If you ask for an autograph from a star who is currently "hot," you can expect a long wait. If you are fortunate enough to request an autograph before or after someone gets hot, your response time may be shorter.

The value of autographs ranges from $3 to over $3000 depending on the market and the time.

For up-to-date information on autographs and collecting trends, look for guides in your local bookstore, or search the Internet under "autograph collecting."

There are several autograph clubs and organizations that you can join:

International Autograph Collectors Club and Dealers Alliance (IACC/DA)
PO Box 848486
Hollywood FL 33024
www.iacc-da.org

Professional Autograph Dealers Association (PADA)
PO Box 1729
Murray Hill Station
New York NY 10156
888-338-4338

The Manuscript Society
350 N Niagara St
Burbank CA 91505-3648
www.manuscript.org

Universal Autograph Collectors Club (UACC)
PO Box 6181
Washington DC 20044-6181
www.uacc.org

In addition to the five addresses above, there are four more Web sites you can contact:

www.autographs.com
Odyssey Publications
510A S Corona Mall
Corona CA 91719-1420
909-371-7137

Autographs.com is the Web page for Odyssey Publications, the most prolific publisher of autograph information. They publish *Autograph Collector*, an excellent magazine written by experts. They are also responsible for *The Official Collectors 2002 Price Guide*, *Addresses of the Rich and Famous*, and the *Autograph Authentication Guide*.

www.celebritylocator.com

Celebrity Locator is a great Web site that can help you find over 6000 current celebrity addresses. Results are not guaranteed, but this is a great start.

www.autographcentral.com/address_haven.html

Autographs Central is another good gateway for autograph collecting. Containing information on all aspects of the hobby, it is highly educational.

www.rrauction.com
R & R Auctions
3 Chestnut Dr
Bradford NH 03110
888-790-2437

R & R Auctions is a valuable source for information on autograph collecting. Their primary function is the sale of authentic autographs (through auction or online sales), but they also serve to educate their customers. Their Web site has information on authenticating, preserving, and obtaining signatures. Their monthly printed catalog is jam-packed with an incredible wealth of signed items, and easily worth waiting for.
Have fun.

Books

Paperback and Hardcover Books and Pulp Magazines

The evolution of the collectible western book is quite complex.
Near the beginning of the twentieth century, the Old West was passing away, but a whole new genre of entertainment was being born. The

traveling Wild West shows had had their day as Wild Bill Hickok and Annie Oakley had finished their tenure. Wyatt Earp and Bill Hickok Jr. had moved to Hollywood to consult on movies.

Wild Bill, Kit Carson and Jesse James had been the focus of dime store novels penned in the late 1800s and early 1900s. Fictional characters such as Red River Bill, Deadshot Dave, Young Wild West, and Roaring Ralph Rockwood (the Reckless Ranger!) also "lived" courtesy of the early pulp fiction market

The frontier spirit had possessed American youth, and "Go west, young man" was the phrase of the day. The west was open, and adventure was everywhere.

Naturally, the cowboy life and its associated struggles were fertile ground for fiction. Hollywood and the silent film industry commemorated the western life with films that starred Tim McCoy, Tom Mix, William S. Hart, Harry Carey and Fred Thompson. The western film had been born.

Hopalong Cassidy was born in the fertile imagination of Clarence E. Mulford in 1907. His Hopalong was foul-mouthed, with a limp, and was not the saint that Bill Boyd portrayed on-screen.

Found in hardcover for the first quarter of the century were the Hopalong Cassidy novels, Zane Grey novels, and the works of many well-known authors.

For over 30 years, grown-up western fans ate up pulp fare for lunch, listened to *Gunsmoke* on the radio during supper and watched "A" westerns on the big screen at night, while the youth read Big Littles, listened to *The Lone Ranger*, and watched Gene Autry and Roy Rogers beat up the bad guys during the Saturday matinee.

With the success of characters like the Shadow and Doc Savage in the pulp magazines, westerns, too, found a home there. With titles like *Blazing Six Guns*, *Western Story Magazine*, *The Rio Kid*, *The Masked Rider*, *The Lone Ranger*, *Wild West Weekly*, *Brave and Bold*, *Zane Grey Westerns*, *Buck Jones Western Stories*, and *.44 Westerns*, interest in the genre was strong. Many writers cut their teeth on the pulps before going on to the more accepted paperback and hardcover market.

Pulp magazines were a phenomenon unto themselves. Named for the cheap paper used (high in pulp content), the pulps provided adventure and escape, from their beginning in 1860 to their lingering end. Colorful covers, multipart stories, emerging authors, and appealing titles characterized this cultural phenomenon.

Once plentiful in supply, these doorways to adventure are becoming scarce. Finding copies in good condition is very difficult due to the high acid content of the paper and covers, which resulted in rapid deterioration. As they were considered trash by many people, millions of copies were destroyed by paper drives and even by well-meaning parents. Good collections are hard to find, and when found, they are rapidly dispersed. (See the next section for further comments about grading an item's condition.)

Since 1938, paperbacks have been part of every reader's world. L. A. Bantam first experimented with the paperback format in a limited 28-book series that included such characters as the Shadow, the Lone Ranger, and Tarzan. Prior to this time, hardcovers and pulp magazines were the only available reading formats.

As the paperback novel gained popularity, publishers such as Ace, Avon, Bantam, Dell, Crest, Gold Medal, Gunfire Western Novels (Hillman), Pocket Books, Pyramid, Signet and others joined the western parade.

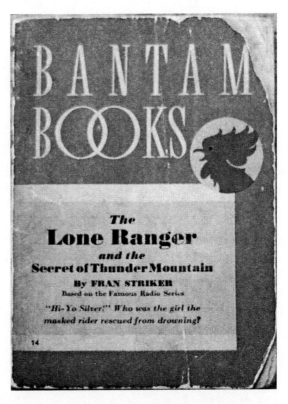

Lone Ranger Bantam 14 (1938), poor condition.

Assuring the success of the western novel were the numerous writers who became established and even beloved in the field. Zane Grey, Ernest Haycox, Luke Short, Max Brand (Frederick Faust), William Hopson, Nelson C. Nye, William Colt MacDonald, B. M. Boumer, Norman A. Fox, Paul Evan Lehman, William Macleod Raine, Wayne D. Overholser, Walker A. Tompkins, Louis L'Amour, W. C. Tuttle, Arthur Henry Gooden, Ray Hogan, Will Ermine, E. B. Mann, Jackson Cole, Al Cody, Clay Fisher, Charles Snow, and more recently Ralph Compton, Elmore Leonard, and Larry McMurtry all experienced popularity at one time or another. Many best sellers became popular movies for Roy Rogers, Gene Autry, Audie Murphy, John Wayne. Some became TV mini-series, such as *Lonesome Dove*.

Into the late '70s, westerns were easily found on the shelves of good booksellers. Today the selection of westerns is more limited. Louis L'Amour, Larry McMurtry, Zane Grey, Ralph Compton, Elmore Leonard,

Elmer Kelton, Matt Braun, Ralph Cotton, William W. Johnstone, Jason Manning, Judson Grey, Charles G. West, Will James, Terry Johnston, the "Spur" and "Longarm" (Tabor Evans) series, Max Brand and only a few others can be found on the shelves.

Hardcovers have been the mainstay of the western genre. Issued from the beginning of the print industry, they have varied little in basic format, but an evolution in materials has occurred.

Binding materials started with linen and have moved to modern adhesives. Edging has evolved from gilt to nothing. Paper has evolved from primitive formulations to the acid-free fibers of today. Dust jackets, now common, have replaced embossing. Frontispieces and other artwork, once standard, now are rarely found in new novels.

Through it all, the western is hanging on.

BIG LITTLE BOOKS

Big Little Books were the first type of print collectible.

Starting in 1933 with the publication of books about Dick Tracy, Little Orphan Annie, and Mickey Mouse, the Whitman publishing company ruled the book shelves with such popular characters as the Shadow, Gene Autry, Tarzan, Buck Rogers, Tom Mix, Captain Midnight, Roy Rogers, the

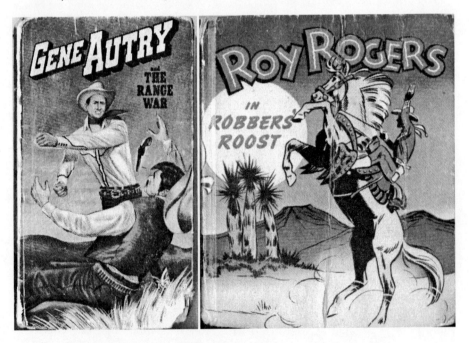

Better Little Books featuring Gene Autry and Roy Rogers.

Lone Ranger, Ken Maynard, Blondie, Buck Jones, George O'Brien, Kit Carson, and a host of others.

Seeing the success of Whitman, other publishers entered the highly profitable juvenile publishing industry. Saalfied Publishing Company picked up the rights to Shirley Temple and produced a flood of popular books. Fawcett, Dell, Blue Ribbon, Engel Van Wiseman, Goldsmith, David McKay, World Syndicate, and Lynn also produced material for the juvenile market.

Highly sought after, this type of book is becoming more rare as supplies dry up. Like the pulp magazines, they were printed on acidic paper. As a result, books in premium condition are difficult to find and even harder to keep that way unless you take the proper steps. (See Chapter 8 for tips on preservation.)

The success of Big Little Books led to many related formats. Better Little Books, Books for Little Hands, Big Big Books, Dime Action Books, Fast-Action Books, Nickel Books, Penny Books, Top-Line Comics, Wee Little Books, and Pop-up Books all had success for many decades.

Grading of Big Little formats (and paperbacks as well) ranges from poor (heavily damaged and soiled) to mint (perfect in every way, glossy cover, white pages, and tight, square spine and corners). Most books are found in good to very good condition and can be purchased for a few dollars. Grading is relatively subjective and should be done by a couple of collectors over a cup of coffee, but the general principles are as follows:

Mint (M): Perfect in every way; white pages, square corners and spine with no rolling. Cover still has original gloss with no color flecks missing and is without marking. Almost impossible to find.

Near Mint (NM): Almost perfect; white pages, mostly square corners and spine; cover still has most of the original cover gloss. A complete book.

Very Fine (VF): Most cover gloss retained with minor wear appearing at corners and around edges; binding still square and tight with no pages missing.

Fine (F): Slight wear starting to show. Cover gloss reduced but still clean; pages still mostly fresh and white; minor spine and corner splits; relatively flat.

Very Good (VG): A reader copy with faded cover luster. Cover is faded but not soiled. Minor corner splits, rolled spine, pages slightly yellowing with none missing.

Good (G): An average used complete copy with minor pieces missing from the book. Corners and spine may be partially split; cover may be marked and faded with slight soiling. Tape damage or repairs may be present.

Fair (Fr): Very heavily read and soiled with small cover chunks missing.
   Spine may be partially missing or rolled.
Poor (P): Damaged, soiled, weathered book unsuitable for collecting.

   Pricing information can be found in the *Overstreet Price Guide Updates* and *Big Little Books: A Collector's Reference and Value Guide* as well as in the dedicated character price guides, and the Big Little Book Web site price guide found at www.ulink.com. The online price guide is an excellent resource for information on the hobby, including pricing, grading, and a list of other resources.
   Another good Web site featuring the history of Big Little Books and a comprehensive listing of the books is found at: www.biglittlebooks.com. Links to other western publishing products are also included.

Western Publishing and Grosset & Dunlap

   Another highly collected format, similar in content to the Big Little Book, is the Whitman series published by Western Publishing, who controlled of Whitman. From the early 1940s until the late 1960s, this giant

Gene Autry Whitman books.

of the industry presented attractively bound and decorated hardcovers targeted for the young at heart. Roy Rogers, Gene Autry, Captain Midnight, Smiling Jack, Tarzan, Dale Evans, Red Ryder, Dick Tracy, and many more newspaper strip characters made the jump to the "Big" books. Television stars were often featured in their own Whitman edition, with the Beverly Hillbillies, Rawhide, the Cartwrights, Lucy, Annie Oakley, the *Have Gun Will Travel* gang, Maxwell Smart, Rin Tin Tin, and other popular characters gracing their covers. Immensely popular, many editions were still being reprinted ten years after their first appearance!

What makes these books unique is their covers. The books were published with either a profusely illustrated dust jacket or, in the case of later editions, with photo laminate covers. The Roy Rogers and Gene Autry series featured good artwork, often with a circular cameo in one of the corners. Each edition had a different dust jacket, thus ensuring the collectibility of each version.

The books themselves also had different color binding for subsequent editions. Green, blue, red, purple, and brown were used to differentiate the books.

Whitman, in addition to their hardcovers, published an extensive col-

Roy Rogers Whitman books.

lection of western star coloring, paint books and paper doll books. Even Roy Rogers and the Lone Ranger could be "dressed up"! These items were well used and well loved by children of the 1940s and 50s. Consequently, their value is high if found unused and uncut.

Grosset & Dunlap is another popular publisher of character-related novels. Publishing since the early part of the 1900s, they presented such popular characters as Tarzan and the Lone Ranger to millions of children over several decades. Usually hardcover, the novels featured colorful dust jackets. The dust jackets rarely survived the years of abuse, so an edition with an intact dust jacket is worth more than one without.

Popular authors published by Grosset & Dunlap include Zane Grey, Maxwell Grant, Edgar Rice Burroughs, Fran Striker, Agatha Christie, William S. Hart, Earl Der Biggers, and many more.

The Lone Ranger novels, like Western's Whitman series, utilized different dust jackets for each printing. The familiar red costume was replaced on covers by the more modern blue after the premiere of the television series (1950). Starting with *The Lone Ranger* (credited to "Gaylord Du Bois"), Fran Striker penned seventeen more novels, ending with *The Lone Ranger on Red Butte Trail*. Paul Laune supplied the interior art for the series from 1941 to the last of the eighteen novels in 1956.

In the case of the immensely popular Tarzan and other Edgar Rice Burroughs novels, Allen St. John provided the interior and dust jacket artwork. Reprinted numerous times, each Tarzan novel is distinguishable by the color of binding, the last novel listed in the "novels by" section, and the number of pages. True first editions are difficult to identify, and a Tarzan price guide should be consulted.

Lone Ranger novels published by Grosset & Dunlap.

A MASKED RIDER SCATTERED THE ANGRY CROWD

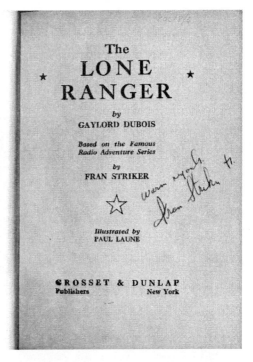

The
★ LONE ★
RANGER

by
GAYLORD DUBOIS

*Based on the Famous
Radio Adventure Series*

by
FRAN STRIKER

☆

Warm regards
from Striker Jr.

Illustrated by
PAUL LAUNE

GROSSET & DUNLAP
Publishers   New York

Rare 1936 "Gaylord Dubois" Lone Ranger (later credited to Fran Striker). Note Fran Striker Jr. autograph. Illustration by Paul Laune.

Whereas Western Publishing (through the Whitman series) focused on the youth market, Grosset & Dunlap presented a wider variety of authors and character series designed to appeal to older age groups as well. Their offerings range from juvenile series (Lone Ranger, Bobbsey Twins) to series by well established authors like Zane Grey.

Other publishers that entered the juvenile and western markets include Simon & Schuster (Little Golden Books), Saalfield Publishing (Will Rogers novels), and Lynn Publishing (Big Little Book format).

In terms of collecting, first editions, complete series, variant covers and colors, autographs, and the presence or absence of dust jackets make a book edition valuable. As each title has a different value, and each author and publisher had varying market demands, contemporary price guides or reputable dealers should be consulted for further information.

Price guides include the *Official Price Guide to Radio TV and Movie Memorabilia*, the *Official Price Guide to Collectible Books*, the *Whitman Juvenile Books: Reference and Value Guide*, and various character related guides. Online, you can consult eBay for prices realized from identical items; or visit www.abe.com and check out similar editions for sale.

Tonto outfit. (Photograph courtesy the Antique Cowboy, www.antiquecowboy.com)

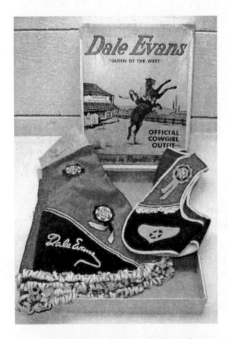

Dale Evans clothing set. (Photograph courtesy the Antique Cowboy, www.antiquecowboy.com)

Costumes

For a true, dyed in the wool front-row kid, the next best thing to owning a gun like your hero was to dress like your hero. From head to toe, cowboy hat to boots, badge to bandana, you could be Roy, the Ranger, Tonto, Zorro, Dale, Hopalong, or Annie. All it took was the right clothes, the right gun, and the right attitude.

Browsing through the Roy Rogers merchandising list, you can find many types of clothing that Roy and Dale graced, including jeans, gloves, shirts, skirts, jackets, socks, hats, boots, slippers, belts, pajamas, chaps, badges— and, for those really cold days on the range, mittens, scarves and toboggan hats.

Hopalong Cassidy (1950s), Roy Rogers, Bat Masterson (1958), Buck Jones, Buffalo Bill Jr., The Cisco Kid (1950s), Dale Evans, Tom Mix, the Lone Ranger (1939 and 1942), Hoot Gibson (1935), Wyatt Earp, Matt Dillon, the Texas Rangers, Wild Bill Hickok, and even Henry Fonda were featured on various costume sets, badges, boots, spurs, chaps, or bandannas. Costumes were sold in sets of up to nine pieces, but individual items were often available and are much more commonly found today. Complete sets in mint condition can bring premium prices (up to $750 or more). Badges, bandannas, cowboy boots, and hats by themselves can bring as little as $20 or as much as the price of a full costume set, depending on the item, character, and condition.

Even the boxes themselves can be valuable. Due to the popularity of the

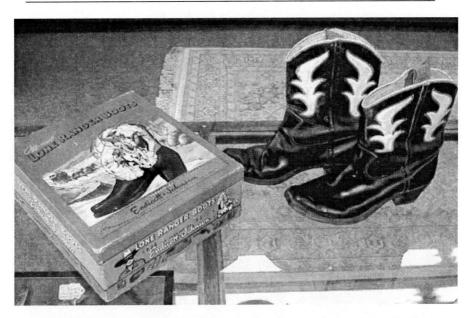

Lone Ranger boots and box. (Photograph courtesy the Antique Cowboy, www.antiquecowboy.com)

clothing items (Roy Rogers had his own clothing line during the 1950s), the boxes sometimes outlasted the clothes. Several Lone Ranger cowboy boot boxes and several Roy Rogers boxes have appeared recently on eBay.

Although it's not the same type of collectible as vintage costumes, many western fans enjoy assembling a wardrobe of Western-style clothing — and in that realm there is nothing more desirable than a "Nudie." One of the most famous clothiers in Hollywood History, James Nudie (always called simply "Nudie") dressed the stars for decades. His trademark glitz adorned suits have been worn by Roy Rogers, Elvis Presley, Clayton Moore (Lone Ranger costume), Marty Stuart, Porter Wagoner, and Elton John. Today, his family carries on the tradition and caters to stars and fans alike. They can be found on the Internet at www.nudierodeotailor.com/index.html.

A popular collectible is the Texas Ranger badge. Such badges are frequently advertised as authentic and "antique" on eBay and in other auctions, but buyers have sometimes been misled and have inadvertently purchased replicas. Authentic badges can be purchased and are sold with Certificates of Authenticity. Replica badges are considered illegal in Texas as the reproductions are sometimes too close to the originals.

A similar situation exists for the Lone Ranger scout badge. In the early 1990s, "original" badges turned up, only to be revealed as modern replicas.

Knowledge of the industry and current awareness of scams are indispensable tools for the wise collector.

Toy auctions, eBay, Amazon, Hake's, the Antique Cowboy (www.antiquecowboy.com) and private dealers are the best sources for costumes and clothing items.

Character Related Publications

Newspaper Strips

Newspaper strips predate comic books. Since the late 1800s, various types of strips have entertained the daily reader. Some became so popular that movies, radio plays, novels, and even TV series were spin-offs.

Comic strips became the first comic books. Publishers, wanting to cash in on the popularity of their characters, collected the daily strips into a single book or a series of books for sale.

"Feature Books," published by David McKay, collected the most popular strips into 68-, 76-, and 100-page black and white formats. King of the Royal Mounted, Popeye, Dick Tracy, Little Orphan Annie, The Lone Ranger, Mandrake the Magician, Flash Gordon and many others thrilled the youth of America for 57 issues until 1948.

The collector of strips has a challenge. The paper used in newspapers is pulp and therefore subject to rapid deterioration due to acid content. Thoughtful collectors saved their beloved strips in low light, low humidity, and medium temperature, and have prolonged the life of their collectibles. (See Chapter 8 for tips on preservation.)

Some collectors store entire pages in mylar sleeves, while others clip out just the strip they need with a ¼" border on either side.

As for Sunday strips, which are far different now than in the past, clipping just the desired section with a border can be done. With Sunday strips older than 20 years, the bonus is often what is on the opposite side! *The Lone Ranger* often backed *Red Ryder*, *Roy Rogers* or *Life with Father*. Some full page Sundays, such as the Tarzan, Prince Valiant and even Phantom strips, were for almost 20 years backed by two other classic strips as well.

In terms of comic strip sources, there are several options. You can collect the strips from the original source (daily newspapers), from a library (often libraries will allow patrons to clip newspapers when they convert their archives to film or electronic storage media), or from eBay, or you can purchase the strips in reprint form from Ken Pierce Books (see below for the address).

Ken Pierce has done a great job of collecting comic strips and reprinting them in a continuous storyline. Westerns, science fiction, drama, and popular mainstream characters are featured in their own softbound books. They can be ordered from:

> Ken Pierce Books
> PO Box 320125
> Franklin WI 53231
> 414-529-3056
> www.kenpiercebooks.com

Another good source for information is Jim Harmon, author of several books on newspaper strips, radio drama and comedy: He can be contacted at:

> Jim Harmon
> 634 S Orchard Dr
> Burbank CA 91506

Additionally, *Andy Madura Sunday Comics and Paper Collectibles* has extensive holdings of Sunday and daily comic strips. Collectors information such as grading and preservation is also presented. He can be contacted at:

> Andy Madura Sunday Comics and
> Paper Collectibles
> Box 526
> New Brunswick Rd
> Somerset NJ 08873
> www.oldsundaycomics.com

Given the tremendous variety of comic strips over the years, there still is an incredible wealth of material to choose from. With the advent of the Internet, there are several Web sites containing over 150 daily strips! *The Phantom, Tarzan, Mandrake the Magician, Dick Tracy, Popeye* and several other strips have made the 50 year mark and continue unabated. Sources for comic strips include:

> www.kingfeatures.com
> (The Phantom, Mandrake the Magician)

> www.unitermedia.com/comics
> (Tarzan)

> www.creators.com

Each Web site will have some duplication, but all told, you can see the best, worst, and the most popular comics, editorials, and columnists from all over the globe.

As a final note, the last western adventure–themed comic strip was *Zorro*, written by Don McGregor and illustrated by Tom Yeates. *Tumbleweed* by Tom Ryan is still in syndication, and entertains fans all over the world.

COMIC BOOKS

Comic books are fun.

Starting from the first real comic book published in 1934 by Eastern Color for Dell, Famous Funnies sold out quickly and became the first monthly series. New Fun (later More Fun 1934) was issued by National Periodical Publications (DC) as well as Detective Comics (1937) and, of course, Action Comics (1938). Early comic series were collections of newspaper strips, some of which later starred in their own titles. Western Picture Stories (1937) was published by The Comics Magazine Company and was one of the first single-themed titles available.

With the arrival of Superman (1938), The Lone Ranger (1939), Batman (1939), Wonder Woman (1940), the Submariner (1940), Captain America (1941), Captain Marvel (1941), and other costumed heroes, the comic book marketplace exploded. Heroes, heroines, teams, and villains were everywhere.

In the western comic book, cowboys were among the first heroes, as movie characters soon found their way to the comics. A partial listing of western heroes and their first appearance follows.

Allan Ladd (1949)
Andy Devine (1950)
Annie Oakley (1953)
Bob Steele (1950)
Buck Jones (1950)
Buffalo Bill (1909)
Buffalo Bill Jr. (1956)
Champion (1950)
Cheyenne (1956)
The Cisco Kid (1950
Dale Evans (1948)
Durango Kid (1949)
Gabby Hayes (1948)
Gene Autry (1941)

Gunsmoke (1956)
Have Gun Will Travel (1958)
Hoot Gibson (1950)
Hopalong Cassidy (1943)
John Wayne (1949)
Johnny Mack Brown (1950)
Ken Maynard (1936)
Lash LaRue (1949)
Lone Ranger (1939)
Maverick (1958)
Monte Hale (1946)
Randolph Scott (1949)
Range Rider (1952)
Red Ryder (1940)

Rawhide (1959)
Rex Allen (1951)
The Rifleman (1959)
Rocky Lane (1949)
Rod Cameron (1950)
Roy Rogers (1944)
Sergeant Preston (1951)
Silver (1952)
Smiley Burnette (1950)
Sunset Carson (1949)
Tex Ritter (1950)
Texas Rangers (1952)

Tim Holt (1948)
Tim McCoy (1948)
Tim Tyler (1948)
Tom Mix (1937)
Tonto (1951)
Trigger (1951)
Whip Wilson (1949)
Wild Bill Elliot (1950)
Will Rogers (1950)
Young Eagle (1950)
Zorro (1949)

Western comics are highly desirable. In addition to the appeal of the character, many comics feature a cover photo of the star. The Dell and Fawcett issues also offered a photo back cover, and special features that included special messages from the star. The covers were not always found anywhere else and often were collected as posters.

Many companies adapted movies to comic books. These issues featured early western stars. Comics such as Dell Four Color, Wow Comics,

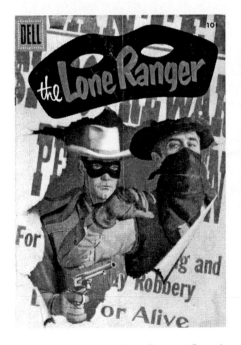

Lone Ranger, Gene Autry, from Dell Comics.

Roy Rogers (no. 139) (note Dusty) from Dell Comics. *Hopalong Cassidy* from Fawcett Comics'.

Prize Comics Western, Feature Films, Motion Picture Comics, True Movie and Television, Movie Comics and Fawcett Movie Comics presented illustrated movies. Bill Black, publisher of AC Comics, has continued this tradition with reprinted adaptations of movie and TV episode featuring classic western stars.

In addition to movie, television, and radio stars making the jump to comic books, original heroes were created by Marvel, DC, Fawcett, and other publishers.

Characters such as the Two Gun Kid, Kid Colt, Rawhide Kid, Ghost Rider, the Ringo Kid, Night Rider, Lone Rider, Jonah Hex, Jesse James, and Johnny Thunder captured the imagination of readers. Some characters remained the same until they faded away; others have changed and have successfully been transformed into modern heroes. (Once a mysterious rider righting the wrongs in the early west, the Ghost Rider now rides a motorcycle sporting a flaming skull and hellfire!)

Comic books are graded via the OWL Card (for page whiteness), the condition system (Poor to Mint), or the ONE Card (Overstreet Number Equivalent).

The OWL card compares page whiteness to an industry standard.

Autographed *Rex Allen* and *Lone Ranger* Silver Anniversary Issue, both from Dell Comics.

(Because comic books are printed on acidic paper, they turn yellow over time. So the whiteness of a page is a good measure of a comic's physical condition.) The ONE Card grading ranges from 1 to 100, where poor is 1 and Mint is 100. The Overstreet Price Guide lists both the abbreviation (PR to MT) and the ONE code.

AC Comics Modern Tribute Editions.

Rawhide Kid no. 93, autographed by the artist, Marvel Comics Group.

Overall grading is similar to the Big Little Books:

Mint (MT) (ONE 100–98): Only subtle binder or printing defects are allowable. Flat cover, no surface wear, bright cover inks and minimal fading characterize these covers. Square corners, clean and centered staples (rust free) and a flat spine are required.

Near Mint (NM) (ONE 97–90): Only minor imperfections allowed. Almost perfect in every way. White pages, square corners and spine with no rolling. Cover still has original gloss with few color flecks missing and mostly without marking. Almost impossible to find.

Very Fine (VF) (ONE 89–75): A visually appealing cover. Most cover gloss retained with minor wear appearing at corners and around edges. Staples may show color bleed. The spine should be almost perfectly flat. Pages and cover may be slightly yellowed or tannish in appearance.

Fine (F) (ONE 74–55): An above-average copy with slight wear starting to show; cover gloss reduced but still clean; pages still mostly fresh and white; minor spine and corner creases; relatively flat.

Very Good (VG) (ONE 54–35): A reader copy with faded cover luster (but not soiled); minor corner splits, rolled spine, pages slightly yellowing with allowable tears or missing pieces. Staples may be loose. Cover may be loose, but not detached. Common bindery flaws and ink marks do not affect the grade.

Good (GD) (ONE 34–15): An average used complete copy with minor pieces missing from the book; corners and spine may be partially split; cover may be marked and faded with slight soiling. Tape damage or repairs may be present. Comics in this condition are marginally collectible.

Fair (FR) (ONE 14–5): A largely complete issue (center fold can be missing), very heavily read and soiled with allowable cover chunks (small) and coupons missing. Spine may be partially missing or rolled. Great for reading, but not recommended for collecting.

Poor (PR) (ONE 4–1): Comics in this condition have no collector value.

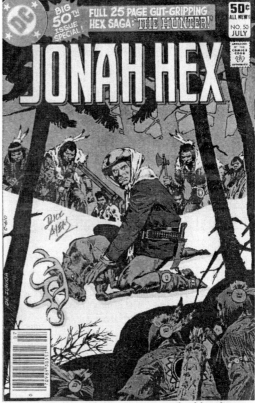

DC Comics' *Jonah Hex*, autographed by the artist.

They may be defaced, missing pages, missing covers, stained, water damaged, or unreadable. Not collected unless the issue is a platinum or key issue.

Where can we find comic books?

Look around. New issues can be purchased at local quick marts, comic stores (also a source for back issues, trade volumes, and other related items), bookstores, or over the Internet (on subscription services).

Back issues (non-current issues) can be purchased at many more venues. Internet retailers offer a complete line of comics, books, toys, magazines, and related paraphernalia.

Conventions offer the collector an excellent opportunity to trade, sell or buy missing issues as well as to meet others with an interest in comics. Professional artists, writers, publishers, and promoters often appear at comic conventions to promote their products and to sign their work. Other collectors are often willing to swap or sell unwanted duplicate issues from their collections.

Comic books can be found on the Internet at various sites. Here are just a few:

www.milehighcomics.com

www.heritagecomics.com

www.accomics.com

AC Comics
Box 5212126
Longwood FL 32752-1216

www.wizardworld.com

www.eBay.com

What makes a comic collectible? Different collectors look for different things. Some collect the works of particular artists or writers. Others look for certain characters. Still others collect according to type of cover (photo, "shock"), publisher (Dell, DC, Marvel, Charlton, Timely, Atlas, Fox, EC), theme, and so on. Photo covers, first appearances, crossovers, deaths, printing flaws, condition, autographs and variant covers add value for the collector.

For in-depth information on comic book collecting, pricing, market trends, buying and selling, consult the *Overstreet Comic Book Price Guide* or the *Comic Values* annual available from Krause Publications. A good comprehensive comic book site on the Internet is www.ComicBookWebsites.com, featuring comic book histories, creators' Web pages, dealers and so much more.

Wizard, a magazine published by Gareb Shamus Enterprises, runs monthly and includes news, views, movie and book reviews, top 10 lists, and current price listings for common post–1963 issues. *Wizard* can be found at your local retailer or purchased online. Online price listings can be found at www.wizardworld.com.

The *Comic Buyers Guide* is the bible of the comic book industry. Published bi-weekly, it is jam-packed with items of interest to collectors and comics fans: artwork, interviews, comic strips, reviews, weekly columns, comic book listings for platinum to silver age issues, and much, much more. You can contact the publishers at

Comic Buyers Guide
700 E State St
Iola WI 54990-0001
800-258-0929
www.krause.com

or purchase the guide at your favorite comic book store.

Cups, Plates and Utensils

Cups, bowls, and utensils were natural for character promotions. What better way to remember your favorite hero than to eat from a Hoppy bowl, drink from a Hoppy cup, and use a Hoppy knife and fork?

The Lone Ranger made an appearance in the kitchen on cups (1938, 1939, 1982), on plates, and on saucers (1939). Roy Rogers and Dale Evans were table guests in the 1950s courtesy of Universal, on plates both metal and ceramic. Hopalong Cassidy made sure kids drank their milk and finished their suppers during the 1950s.

Food plates and accessories rarely survived the handling they received. As a result, they are rare and sought after, and their value is high in good condition. Further information can be found in the *Official Hake's Price Guide to Character Toys.*

Right: Bonanza tin cups, 1960s. *Above*: Roy Rogers and Dale Evans plate and cup set. (Photograph courtesy the Antique Cowboy, www.antiquecowboy.com)

reverse
side of
mug

Lone Ranger mugs.

Commemorative Weapons

COMMEMORATIVE WEAPONS AND PLAY SETS

Toy guns were among the earliest of playthings. First appearing in the 1850s, they were popular right into the 1960s. Today, few toy guns can be found in the stores. Space weapons have taken the place of western pistols and rifles. In North America, toy guns now have to be sold with orange caps on the ends for safety.

Commemorative weapons like rifles and pistols are still issued for mature collectors. Harry Carey Jr. (Investment Arms issue 2000), Roy Rogers (A & A Engraving 2000), Rex Allen, and Gabby Hayes have been honored with special editions created just for them.

America Remembers has a complete line of commemorative weapons. Rifles and pistols are created in remembrance of the western greats. Stars such as Audie Murphy, Bruce Boxleitner, Buffalo Bill, Clayton Moore, Clint Walker, C. M. Russell, Cochise, Dale Berry, Dennis Weaver, Gene Autry, Smiley Burnette, Gabby Hayes, Herb Jeffries, Hopalong Cassidy, Iron Eyes Cody, James Arness, Monte Hale, Rex Allen, Roy Rogers, Dusty Rogers, Wyatt Earp and other historical figures are represented by issues. Superbly decorated stocks and barrels characterize this company's work.

For more information on working commemorative weapon issues, you can contact:

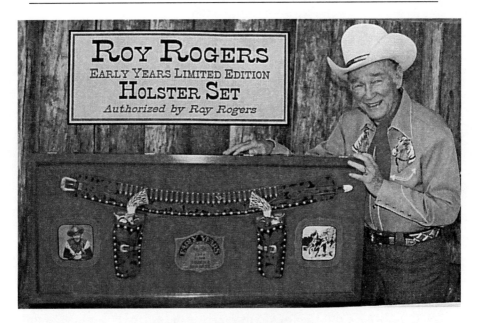

Roy Rogers Early Years Holster Set.

Investment Arms Inc
4631 S Mason
Ste B3
Fort Collins CO 80525
888-708-4867
www.investmentarms.com

A & A Engraving Inc
807 E Andrew St
Rapid City SD 57701
605-343-7640
www.aaengraving.com

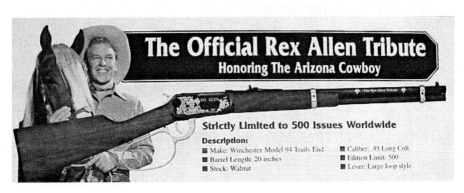

Box for Rex Allen issue. (Courtesy America Remembers®)

Rex Allen issue. (Courtesy America Remembers®)

America Remembers
10226 Timber Ridge Dr
Ashland VA 23005
804-550-9616
Fax: 804-550-9603
www.americaremembers.com

Daisy Manufacturing has issued a three-gun commemorative set featuring Roy Rogers, Dale Evans, and Gabby Hayes. The production run was limited to 2500 for each model, and all quickly sold out. The Red Ryder Daisy BB rifle is still sold in North America and is largely considered to be the most popular rifle ever produced.

Early toy guns were made of cast iron until World War II cut off the material supply. Toy makers turned to die cast metals with plastic embellishments during the 1950s, and today plastic is used almost exclusively in the less expensive toys. Commemorative sets still use real metal, but children generally do not have access to these models.

As in the case of books and comics, licensed characters appeared on pistol sets. Buffalo Bill made his first appearance on a gun way back in 1890! In 1925, 1930, and 1940 he also graced the barrel and stock of a firearm.

The list of licensed products includes:

Billy the Kid (1938), Stevens   Gene Autry (1939, 1940), Kenton
Buffalo Bill (1890), Stevens   Hopalong Cassidy (1950s),
Daniel Boone Derringer, Marx   Wyandotte and Schmidt

Roy Rogers and Dale Evans BB gun.

Kit Carson (1928), Kenton

Lone Ranger (1939), Kilgore, Marx

Lone Ranger Miniature Collection (1939, unknown)

Lone Ranger (1970s and 80s, unknown)

Roy Rogers (1940), Hubley and Kilgore

Buffalo Bill Jr. pistol, ca. 1950s.

Gun sets were commonly manufactured in the early part of the century. By the mid-century mark, only a few manufacturers were left. Kilgore, Hubley, Stevens, Kenton, Wyandotte, Marx and Daisy produced toy guns for the boomer generation.

Rarely found in original packaging, or even in working order, toy pistols or rifles in premium condition can fetch hundreds of dollars. If you consider the fact that holsters and gun belts were sometimes part of the sets, a complete rig is even more difficult to find.

Roy Rogers pistol and holsters. (Photograph courtesy the Antique Cowboy, www.antiquecowboy.com)

Some things to consider when grading gun sets or rifles:

1. Is the set in working order? Working guns have more value.
2. Is the set complete? Complete sets are more desirable.
3. Is the set marked in any way? Is there damage to any part of the set that is beyond repair? (Owner's "tattoos," unless the owner is a star, devalue the item.)
4. Presence or absence of original packaging. With original packaging, like models, "Mint in Box" (MIB) brings premium price.
5. Relative rarity of item. Rare items bring premium price.
6. Character identity or toy manufacturer. The complete Roy Rogers Kilgore set brings hundreds of dollars, while a complete generic Marx may bring only $50.

Flea markets, garage sales, estate auctions, eBay auctions, and, of course, dedicated toy auctions are among the best sources for toy guns and gun sets.

Information on the growing hobby of gun collecting can be found from a variety of sources. *Gun Report Magazine, Antique Toy World Magazine,* the *Official Hake's Price Guide to Character Toys, Cast Iron Toy Guns* (by Charles Best), and *Cast Iron Toy Pistols* (also by Charles Best), and *Television's Cowboys, Gunfighters and Their Cap Pistols* (by Rudy D'Angelo) are good reference sources. Gun shows are a great resource for information on toy guns as well as the real things. The contact information for recommended magazines follows:

> *Antique Toy World* (monthly)
> Dale Kelley
> PO Box 34509
> Chicago IL 60634

> *Toy Shop* (bi-weekly)
> Krause Publications
> 700 E State St
> Iola WI 54990

> *Toy Gun Collectors of America Newsletter* (quarterly)
> Jim Buskirk
> 3009 Oleander Ave
> San Marcos CA 92069

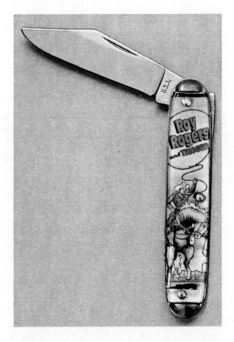

Monte Hale knife and Roy Rogers knife.

Collectible pocket knives can also be found. Stars such as Tom Mix, Roy Rogers, the Lone Ranger, Gene Autry, Davy Crocket, Hopalong Cassidy, Trigger, Dale Evans, and Zorro have been featured on pocket knives. Currently available from the star museums, these items are still relatively popular.

Manufacturers include the Novelty Knife Company (Silver Screen Heroes) and the Smoky Mountain Knife Works (Riders of the Silver Screen). These knives can be found in good memorabilia stores, eBay, or in your favorite movie museum gift shop.

Further information on knife collecting can be found at Cutlers Cove (www.cutlerscove.com) and Smoky Mountain Knife Works (www.eknife-works.com), which are both excellent sources for knife lore.

Toys, Cards, Figurines, Games and Models
COLLECTIBLE CARD SETS

Collectible cards have always been with us as long as there have been westerns. Collectible cards have taken the form of trading cards, bubble gum cards, and the nickel card.

Early card editions were printed on cheap, high-pulp paper and therefore subject to the ravages of acid, humidity and temperature. Later versions were printed on somewhat better paper and sported a glossy finish. Today's cards use low-acid stock, and some are glossy on both sides.

Early character cards could be purchased in arcade-type machines

Cards from Lone Ranger reprint set from the 1980s.

and featured Tim McCoy, John Wayne, Ken Maynard, Roy Rogers, Dale Evans, Gene Autry, and other stars. They are frequently found in fair to good condition. For the 1938 Lone Ranger feature, a series of four cards was issued, featuring Chief Thundercloud (Victor Daniels), Lee Powell, Silver, and one action scene.

The Lone Ranger was again featured in a card series in the early 1940s, and again the late '80s in reprint form. Artwork from the premiums was released in at least a 12-card set. Original cards are hard to find, and the reprints are easy to spot: Instead of faded and yellowed, the artwork in reprints is clean and clear.

In Britain, Roy Rogers Bubble Gum included card (1 ¾" × 2½") series featuring scenes from Roy Rogers movies. From 1955, *South of Caliente* and *In Old Amarillo* were released on photographic paper in 24 card sets. Other issues have not been verified yet.

Roy Rogers again was honored with two sets of cards in the 1990s. Arrowcatch Productions released a Gold Signature 20-card set featuring classic Roy Rogers comic books and personal photographs in 1992. Two sets featuring all the comic book covers were released and sold extremely well.

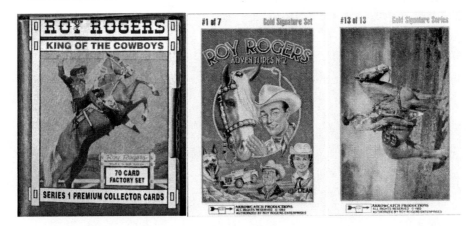

Left: Roy Rogers Comic Cover set of collector cards (1990s). *Center and right*: Arrowcatch Gold Signature set of collector cards (1992).

In 1988, a 40-card "Saturday Serials" set was issued that featured the best of the movie serials. Thirteen serials were included, among them *Zorro Rides Again*, *The Lone Ranger*, and *The Adventures of Captain Marvel*. Each three card section (per serial) featured the title card, chapters, story and two classic images from the film. Issued in small quantities, they are difficult to find.

In 1993, the Smoky Mountain Knife Works issued a 300-card, 44-star set. Featuring poster art, lobby cards, biography cards, and publicity photographs, this set is a must-have for the western collector. Pacific Cards also issued a 110-card *Gunsmoke* set.

The year 1997 saw Dart Flip Cards issue a classy Lone Ranger 72-card set that featured, as a promotion, a signed Fran Striker Jr. card, and a six card die cut limited run.

Smoky Mountain Knife Works set of collector cards, 1993.

**Chief Thundercloud (Victor Daniels)
Trading Cards.**

During the 1960s, trading cards were frequently issued for popular television programs. Westerns were no different, and shows like *Bonanza* and *Gunsmoke* found audiences with kids everywhere.

As with comic books, books, and most collectibles, the value of a card depends partly on its condition:

Mint (M)—A card with no defects, razor sharp corners, even borders, original gloss on the front with a sharp picture, no signs of wear, no printing flaws.

Near Mint (NM)—A card with a very minor defect: light fuzziness on one corner, a small amount of original gloss lost, very minor wear on the edges, slightly off-center borders, minor printing flaw.

Excellent Plus (EX+)—A card with a few minor flaws, but no major defects. Many have minor wear on the edges, small fuzziness on the corners, very small amount of wear, slightly off-center borders, slight fading.

Excellent (EX)—A card with minor defects: some slight rounding at some of the corners, some wear at the edges, off-center borders, some possible visible wear.

Very Good (VG)—A card that has been handled and may have minor creases, rounded corners, scuffing at the borders, slight notches on the edges, off-center borders or discoloration. The gloss of the card may be gone, and the picture may be slightly out of focus.

Good (G)—A card that has been handled a lot and possibly scuffed. There may be rounding or layering at the corners, and the borders may be way off center. Gloss may be lost from the face. Edges may be notched.

Poor (P)—Card may have a tear, writing on it, or a major physical defect.

The better the condition, the higher the value. Other factors that influence the value of a card or card set include completeness of set, rarity and demand for set, presence of autographs, and the present status of the licensed property.

Besides collectible cards, playing cards were also issued. Western stars like Rod Cameron, Roy Rogers, Rex Allen, Rocky Lane and others were featured on playing card decks in the 1950s. Roy was also on a Gemaco Product in the mid–1960s that featured only one image of Roy at the top of the cards.

For more information on this aspect of western collectibles, you can refer to the *Official Hake's Price Guide to Character Toys*, dedicated card magazines such as Krause's *Collectors Magazine & Price Guide*, and a company called *Non Sports Updates*, who can be contacted at

Non Sports Updates
4019 Green St
Harrisburg PA 17110
800-228-9678
www.nonsportsupdate.com

The Trading Card Hobbyist Web site is a good source for current information on new and collectible card sets. They can be found at www.tradingcardhobbyist.com.

FIGURINES

Collectible western figurines are in a growth market. From the first crude figurines of the 1930s to the sophisticated, multi-jointed, multi colored, realistic products we have today, kids have always collected figurines.

Early figurines were produced from a single mold and did not usually have moveable joints. Frequently the figurine, if small, was produced in a single color, and each figurine was hand-painted for fine detail work. Early figures produced included the Lone Ranger and Tonto (1938),Tom Mix and Tony and numerous others.

The 1950s brought Hartland and its vast collection of figurines. Produced in three sizes— 9½", 8", and 5½"— the Hartland issues are well known for their quality. Television and historical characters such as Annie Oakley, Bill Longly, Brave Eagle, Bret Maverick, Buffalo Bill, Cheyenne, Chief Thundercloud, Cochise, Dale Evans, Davy Crockett, George Custer, George Washington, Jim Bowie, Josh Randle, Matt Dillon, Sgt. Lance O' Rourke, Jim Hardie, Roy Rogers, the Lone Ranger, Tonto, Sergeant Preston, Wyatt Earp, Bat Masterson, Paladin, and others were recreated in stunning detail. Bright colors, good production values, and solid construction characterize the Hartland issues.

Highly valued and prized by collectors, premium-condition Hartland figures are becoming increasingly difficult to find. More often they are found in well-loved condition, commonly missing hats, guns, and horses. As in the case of games, duplicates may have to be purchased to complete a character.

The "Best of the West" collection from Marx debuted in 1965, following the explosion of Hasbro's G. I. Joe soldier doll. Fort Apache, Bill Buck, Brave Eagle, the Johnny West family (Jane, John, Jamie, Janice, Jay, Josie), the Indians (Chief Cherokee, Fighting Eagle, Geronimo, Princess Wildflower), Thunderbolt (the horse), Sam Cobra, and Zeb Zachary were produced by Marx from 1965 to 1974. In addition to the characters, play forts and stagecoaches were also marketed.

The Marx figurines featured molded high impact plastic complete with fully jointed elbows and knees, spring-supported legs and arms, and an amazing number of accessories.

Johnny West and the "Best of the West" collection are highly prized. Complete character sets with boxes sell for upwards of $100. Marx has begun reissuing select figures from the collections. As of this writing, Johnny West and George Custer are now available at

www.marxtoys.com
3440 Rt 9 S
Freehold NY 07728
800-621-6279

Captain Action made his debut in 1967. Ideal Toys, seeing the bonanza generated by Marx and G. I. Joe, added their unique approach to the mix.

Captain Action was a man of mystery. What's more, Captain Action was naked. To create, a character, you had to purchase the costume for Captain Action. The first two costumes available were the Lone Ranger and Tonto. Later, Ideal offered cos-

Johnny West and Thunderbolt by Marx.
(Author's much-loved childhood toys)

tumes for superheroes such as the Green Hornet and Spiderman. The costumes came with clothes, face mask, and the guns, rifles and necessary accessories.

Collectors value the Captain Action sets. Current demand has increased the price range of kits from $50 to upwards of $6000 (Green Hornet). If you have any originals, keep them. It's better than the stock market.

Faced with complex licensing agreements, Ideal dropped the versatile doll in 1969. However, re-issues of their most popular accessory sets are now available.

As the race to produce superhero figurines opened to new competitors, a company called Mego grabbed the baton and ran. Issuing the "World's Greatest Superheroes" set first, they rapidly expanded their line to include licensed television and movie properties.

In 1973, Mego issued their western set, "The American West." Including Buffalo Bill, Sitting Bull, Cochise, Davy Crockett, Shadow, Wild Bill Hickok, and Wyatt Earp, this collection was supplemented by the Dodge City playset.

Gabriel Toys also leapt into the fray with "The Lone Ranger Rides Again" (1979), and "The Legend of the Lone Ranger" (1982), based on the movies of the same name. The Lone Ranger, Tonto, Dan Reid, Little Bear, Red Sleeves, Buffalo Bill Cody, Butch Cavendish, General Custer, Scout, Silver, and Smoke were all issued for the young at heart. Play sets such as a fort and a stagecoach were also sold.

Most figurines are found loose and unpackaged. Particularly desirable are items in their original boxes or mounted on their cards. In the case of older Hartland toys, original packaging is extremely rare, and a figure in good condition with all the pieces present is the best you can hope for. With Johnny West and the "Best of the West"

Lone Ranger and Silver. (Author's childhood toys)

sets, more are available in packaging, but most have been played with and pieces have been lost.

Breyer Animal Creations has been manufacturing quality animal models since 1950. Purchased by Reeves International, Inc. in 1984, Breyer is best known for its model horses (made in four different scales) which are produced in porcelain, resin and plastic, and are considered highly collectible.

Breyer offers about 200 different animals each year including horse breeds from around the world, dogs, farm animals and wildlife. Of specific interest to the western collector is the "Hollywood Heroes" series: Silver (574), Scout (1122), Buttermilk (1123), Champion (1111), Diablo (1152), Spirit (577), Topper (1177), and Trigger (758); all are produced in Breyer's Traditional line in cellulose acetate plastic. Several of the "Heroes" series come with a commemorative video. Trigger is also available in a limited edition porcelain (8125).

For a complete overview of the Breyer product line, go to www.breyerhorses.com, or contact

> Breyer Horses
> Division of Reeves International
> 14 Industrial Rd
> Pequannock NJ 07440
> 973-694-5006

Trigger (#758). (Courtesy Breyer Horses)   Silver (#574).

The Web site features a great history, an illustrated online catalog and valuable information on the hobby itself.

For good pricing information there are several sources. *O'Brien's Collectors Toys* has a good figurine section. *Toy Fare*, published by Gareb Shamus Enterprises (which also publishes *Wizard* for comic books), lists contemporary figurine collectibles values; it also features stories on the industry and news about upcoming issues from manufacturers. The various character price guides (*Roy Rogers*, *Lone Ranger* and so on) also list figurine values and usually provide photos of the items. Amazon and eBay also serve as useful references for values of your prized "dolls."

GAMES

Licensed games have been part of western memorabilia collecting since the late 1930s. Board games, target games, and (recently) trivia games are all part of this broad genre of collectibles.

Board games inspired by western stars of movie and television include "The Lone Ranger" (1939, 1981), "Annie Oakley" (1955), "Bat Masterson" (1958), "Bonanza" (1964), "Branded," "Cheyenne" (1958), "Davy Crockett" (1955), "F Troop" (1965), "Have Gun Will Travel" (1959), "Gunsmoke" (1958), "Johnny Ringo" (1960), "Laramie" (1960), "Pony Express" (1960), "Rawhide" (1960), "Rifleman" (1958), "Wild Bill Hickok" (1956), "Wyatt Earp" (1958), and many others too numerous to mention. If there was a television show, there was probably a game for kids to play with.

Target-shooting games, today frowned upon, were commonplace promotional items featuring the likes of the Lone Ranger, Hopalong Cassidy, Cheyenne, Roy Rogers, and Gene Autry.

Board games often featured licensed artwork or photographs of the main character on the box top and game board. Game pieces usually carried through with the game's theme.

Wells Fargo board game.

Board games are difficult to find today. They are often incomplete, and you may have to purchase two or more to get a complete set. Even incomplete, a character game is worth a lot to a true fan — if not for the box artwork (or photo), then just for the sheer enjoyment of feeling like a kid again.

MODEL KITS

Model kits featuring western stars were produced by various manufacturers. Aurora and Pyro manufactured western-themed models from 1958 to the mid–1970s.

Pyro issued "Ghost Rider" (1970), "Wyatt Earp" (1958), "Rawhide" (1958), and "Restless Gun" (1958). Pyro's original molds were purchased by Life-Like in the 1970s and many kits were reissued in the 1980s.

Aurora was the king of model kit manufacturers. From humble beginnings in 1952, Aurora got into the figure kit market in 1955 and, until its demise, produced cutting-edge models that cashed in on the pop icon status the company had achieved. The company was purchased by Nabisco in 1971 and shut down in 1977.

Aurora kits have been reissued in reprinted packaging with the original copyright, new copyright and a UPC code. Aurora kits are identified by the character and the model number.

Western-themed models issued by Aurora include:

Apache Warrior #401 (1961)
Confederate Raider #402 (1959)
George Washington #852 (1965)
Indian Chief #417 (1957)
Indian Squaw #418 (1958)
Jerry West #865 (1965)
Jesse James #408 (1966)

Lone Ranger #808 (1967)
Lone Ranger Comic Scenes #188 (1974)
Tonto #809 (1967)
Tonto Comic Scenes #183 (1974)
Zorro #801 (1965)

With the Comic Scenes models, the value of the model is enhanced by the inclusion of a comic book. Artwork for the series was done by the best comic book artists of the day, such as Neal Adams, Gil Kane, Carmine Infantino, and others. The comics themselves are in high demand even without the model they accompanied.

The value of a model kit is dependent upon several factors. Box condition, rarity of model, presence

Aurora model #183 (1974), Tonto Comic Scenes.

or absence of shrink wrap, degree of assembly, degree of painting, presence or absence of instructions, foreign or domestic version, and the completeness of a kit all affect a model's value.

In terms of models, values for models MIB (Mint in Box) range from $10 to over $1500. Aurora editions bring the highest prices. A general guideline follows ("full price" refers to the highest price shown in current guides):

MIB (Mint in Box) Sealed — Complete in every way. Full price plus.

MIB (Mint in Box) Not sealed — Complete in every way, plastic pieces still attached to frames, no paint or glue on pieces. Full price.

Partial Assembly: Partially assembled model with no paint or glue, full instructions. Styrene glue decreases the value of the model. 80–85 percent of full price.

Partial Painting: Model may be assembled and partially painted. (Experienced collectors can strip paint if necessary.) Complete model kit with instructions. 80 percent of full price.

Partial assembly/painting: Model may be partially assembled and painted, all pieces present. 75 percent of full price.

Built Model: Finished in every way. No box or instructions. 15 to 45 percent of full price.

Missing Pieces: Few collectors want incomplete models. Price declines rapidly with missing pieces. Missing Instructions: Decrease in value of model by 10 percent if instructions are missing from model.

Boxes: Collectible only for the Aurora models. Boxes in good shape can bring up to 40 percent of full price depending on the model.

As in the case of most collectible toys, model kits are most desirable (and expensive) when found in MIB condition. For a good source of pricing and hobby information, check out *Aurora History and Price Guide.*

A good source for model information on the Internet is www.greenmodels.com.

Lunch Boxes and Ornaments

The collecting of lunch boxes is addictive.

Snazzy lunch kits featuring characters such as Roy Rogers, Dale Evans, Gene Autry, the Lone Ranger, Daniel Boone, Zorro, or TV shows such as *The Rifleman, Gunsmoke,* and *Bonanza,* made many trips to school and back. Today, these kits have found their way into collections across North America.

King Seeley and Aladdin produced millions of lunch boxes and vac-

Gunsmoke lunch box, and 1954 Hopalong Cassidy lunch box.

uum bottle sets over three decades. Today, Aladdin and Thermos are the most prominent manufacturers of licensed lunch kits.

Hallmark and other manufacturers have in the recent past reissued commemorative lunch boxes in sizes ranging from miniature to almost full size. The miniatures, intended for Christmas tree ornaments, include the Lone Ranger and Hopalong Cassidy. (Non-western themes include *Star Trek*, *Star Wars*, *The Wizard of Oz*, *Peanuts* and many more.) Both Hallmark and Carlton Cards are active in this field.

Lunch boxes have changed a lot over the years. Construction materials have gone from steel (hinges, top and bottom), to plastic (top and bottom). (Today's lunch kits are often bags though the traditional box design is still available.)

Lone Ranger lunch kits.

Left: Hopalong Cassidy lunch box by Hallmark, 2000. Christmas ornaments: Lone Ranger miniature lunch box and miniature figurine by Hallmark.

The value of lunch boxes is quite varied. With the use (and abuse) that lunch boxes receive, it is rare to even find one in reasonable condition. The value of a lunch box depends on its condition, its completeness, the character, and the market demand. Prices range from $15 (in good condition) for a complete kit up to over $400 for one in high demand and in excellent condition.

Great sources for pricing information are the *Official Hake's Price Guide to Character Toys*, eBay and Amazon on the Internet, and Hakes Americana and Collectibles for print catalog and auctions:

> Hake's Americana & Collectibles
> PO Box 1444K
> York PA 17405
> 717-848-1333
> www.hakes.com

Magazines and TV Guides

Movie or movie star related magazines have always been collectible, and western related movie magazines even more so. Published for a smaller audience, they are today more rare and as a result more prized.

Popular magazines of the day featured western idols on their covers. Roy Rogers (July 12, 1943) and Hopalong Cassidy (June 12, 1950) both appeared on *Life* covers. *Time* also featured Hopalong Cassidy on its cover in 1950. Family magazines played up the wholesome images of the popular cowboys, and fan magazines like *Who's Who in Western Stars* profiled the major stars of the day in each issue.

TV Guide is a gold mine of early television lore and trivia. Initially

Who's Who in Western Stars no. 4, featuring Roy Rogers on the cover. *Life* magazine, June 12, 1950, with Hopalong Cassidy cover.

introduced as a regional magazine (due to the regional nature of television) in 1953, it quickly became a national staple, and it still sells millions of issues weekly. Serving as a listing for movies and television shows, and also a means to promote hot shows, *TV Guide* has become a certifiable collectible itself, thanks to the photo covers (and sometimes the articles).

Of interest to western fans are the covers and issues that feature our heroes. Like comic books, a full set of conditions applies to the grading of *TV Guide* magazines.

The list of appearances by western stars is long, but it includes serial stars. A partial list of *TV Guide* issues up to 1973 (dates, issue number, actor or show) follows.

REGIONAL ISSUES

July 28–August 3, 1951, Buster Crabbe
May 16–22, 1952, Gene Autry
November 6–12, 1953, Warren Hull cover (The Spider)

NATIONAL ISSUES

July 17–23, 1954, Roy Rogers
May 11–17, 1957, issue 215, James Arness

Maverick cover   *Bonanza* cover   *Gunsmoke* cover *TV Guide*

August 31–September 6, 1957, issue 231, Clint Walker
April 5–11, 1958, issue 262, Gale Storm
November 22–28, 1958, issue 295, Ronald Reagan (*Death Valley Days*)
February 7–13, 1959, issue 306, Chuck Connors
August 13–19, 1960, issue 385, Nick Adams
February 9–15, 1963, issue 515, Ernest Borgnine
August 22–28, 1970, issue 908, *Gunsmoke*
January 30–February 5, 1970, issue 931, James Arness
August 14–20, 1971, issue 959, *Bonanza*
December 11–17, 1971, issue 976, James Garner
October 7–13, 1972, issue 519, *Bonanza*
November 4–10, 1972, issue 523, John Wayne
June 30–July 6, 1973 , issue 557, Dennis Weaver

Have Gun Will Travel

The value of a *TV Guide* ranges from $3 to well over $400. The George Reeves issue is extremely rare and considered a gem among collectors. A good *TV Guide* section can be found in the *Magazine Collectibles Price List*. On the web, the TV Guide Specialists feature the most complete collection of *TV Guide* for sale. You can search for issues by articles or cover photographs. They can be contacted at

TV Guide Specialists
PO Box 20 W
Macomb IL 61455
309-833-1809
www.oldtvguides.com

Another source of *TV Guide* issues is:

Lenore Levine
PO Box 246-PG
Three Bridges NJ 08887
908-788-0532

Today, the guides are issued by area. Los Angeles will have its own *TV Guide* with the same cover as Houston, but the listings will change. Multiple covers are also being issued to enhance the collectibility of the magazine. Hang on to them! They may be worth money in the future.

The best source is, of course, *TV Guide* itself. Their Web site includes television listings, archives, episode guides to past shows, and cover scans of issues over the years.

They can be found at www.tvguide.com.

Personal Items

The collection of stars' personal items is a relatively new phenomenon.

With the passing of the western stars, the heirs and estates are now taking to selling assets and personal belongings. We have seen recent major auctions by the Roy Rogers family, the Clayton Moore family, and to a smaller degree the Rex Allen family.

There are several problems with collecting personal paraphernalia.

The first is authenticity. How can you, as a collector, be sure that the actor truly owned or used the item that you have acquired? A Certificate of Authenticity (COA) is helpful, but even that is not a sure sign of authenticity.

Second, the issue of value and pricing comes up. How do we value a personal item used by our heroes in life? By auction? By haggling? High Noon Auctions of Los Angeles, Sotheby's, and Heritage Comics have proven to be reputable sources for values and certified items.

On the passing of Clayton Moore, Sotheby's Auction House was commissioned to disperse the Masked Man's estate. When Roy and Dale galloped on, their estates were sold by High Noon Auctions.

All things considered, owning a piece of clothing or jewelry that Dale Evans wore, a hat that graced Roy's head in *Under Nevada Stars*, or an

actual Lone Ranger cos-
tume would be a high
point in most collectors'
lives. There is only one of
the item — no fakes, no
forgeries. The item will
not be reissued with a
new artwork tag. There is
just one. And it's yours!

At various times in
my collecting life, I have
been offered a Clayton
Moore Lone Ranger cos-
tume and an authentic

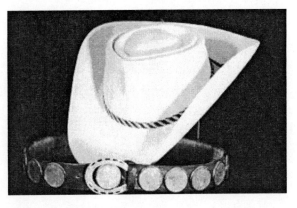

Roy Rogers hat offered by High Noon Auctions.

Rex Allen parade uniform. I traced the source of both items, and both
proved to be authentic.

Movie and Television Props

Early western movie and television props are rare. The first westerns
were produced in the early 1900s. Until the mid–1960s, most movie props
were stored by the studios and reused in various productions. Apart from
re-use the props (buildings, clothing, furniture, and the commonly used
items) were considered to be of little value.

When the early studios were absorbed by the larger organizations,
their warehouses of props and costumes were consolidated into the big
studios' holdings. As a result, there was duplication of many items. Extra
props were either dispersed through sale, hauled off to the garbage dump
or destroyed.

In the early 1970s MGM held a major sale of its costume and prop
inventory. Purchases by collectors included rare *Gone with the Wind*
dresses, cups, plates, furniture and an almost endless list of significant collectibles.

Other studios threw away their stock props and film footage as no
use was found for their archival material. Republic Studios, after re-edit-
ing their film features, threw away the unused film, destroying the original films forever!

Fortunately for collectors, prudent professionals began collecting
movie props directly from the studios. The result is a verifiable product
that is now considered to be a legitimate collectible.

Once the studios caught on to the value of props as collectibles, they
changed their ways, and today it is easy to find current movie props for

sale. Sony, MGM, Universal, and Dream Works regularly hold auctions of their props and costumes. A Certificate of Authenticity is included with each item to guarantee their pedigree as a collectible both archival and historically valuable.

Prop auctions are held online at the following Web sites:

www.movieprop.com
(Listings of price guides and great hobby links)

www.highnoon.com
High Noon Auctions
9929 Venice Blvd
Los Angeles CA 90034
310-202-9010

www.webautographs.com
Legends Memorabilia
20235 Fraser Hwy
Langely BC
V3A 4 E7
604-534-1410

www.hollywoodlostandfound.com
(Movie prop sales and auctions)

Western props from classic television shows and movies can be viewed at the Gene Autry Heritage Museum. Guns, costumes, and personal items from the stars are on permanent display while a video screen plays western videos alongside the items. The Roy Rogers museum likewise displays classic movie props from Roy Rogers and Dale Evans movies.

Scripts and Press Packets

Western movie, radio and television scripts and press packets from the golden age of westerns are hard to come by. Like props and movie posters, the scripts used by the production companies and the press kits issued by studios were considered to be of little value. As a result, supplies of original issues are tight. With the copying technology now available, reproductions and forgeries of "authentically" signed copies are more plentiful but worth less than originals.

When a production was complete, scripts were supposed to be returned to the studio for disposal or storage. According to Fred Foy, announcer for the *Lone Ranger* radio series, the scripts were all tossed out. Some, however, found their way into the hands of dealers. Others were retained in studio files. Upon the dismantling of old studios, many press kits, stills, contracts, props, and scripts were snapped up by collectors around the world.

A script is considered original if it was used in the production of the movie. Script covers may be elaborate, mimeographed (in the case of pre–1950 movies), or marked "Studio Xerox" (pre–1960), but are usually printed with colored front pages identifying the production number, title, director, writer, and draft (if applicable).

Copies are less desirable from a purist viewpoint, but are no less enjoyable. A script for *Casablanca* is still enjoyable for its entertainment value, even though it may be just a copy.

Autographs enhance the value of movie and television scripts considerably. An original copy of the *Gone with the Wind* script signed by all of the stars brought in slightly over $2 million in the early 90s in England.

Authentic press kits and scripts will frequently have stamps that state "Property of" or theater notes like "front window display" on them. Production codes can also be found on the bottom of stills included in the press kits.

Press kits include black and white or color production stills, cast listings, story synopses, actor biographies, press releases and contact information. Press kits often contain information not found anywhere else and are therefore of historical value.

Press books are similar in content, but are usually bound. Designed for the promotion of a film, they contain examples of ad copy, photographs, critic's information, clip ads and art.

For scripts, press kits and press books, autographs, the condition of the packaging or binding, the contents (complete or not), the movie association, the cast, and of course your interest in the item all factor into the value. The more popular the movie or star, the higher the value of the script or press kit generally is.

Recording Collectibles

MOVIE AND TV EPISODES

Collecting tapes of movies and TV episodes is a rewarding hobby. Today, with the advent of the Western Channel, Hallmark, Turner Classics, TV Land, and the efforts of the studios and families to restore and preserve the classics, the availability of western material is expanding. With the improvement of digital technology, we are now seeing a large scale restoration of the early films.

Recently, the Roy Rogers estate authorized Sagebrush Entertainment

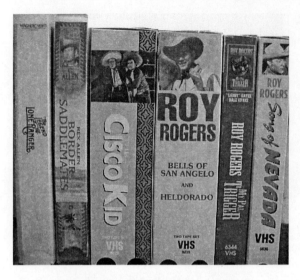

Examples of VHS movies available.

to restore and distribute newly discovered full length Rogers and Evans films as well as Roy Rogers productions. Sagebrush Entertainment also has the task of restoring and distributing the Hopalong Cassidy film and television series productions. The Gene Autry estate has restored and reissued the Gene Autry films and television shows. Paramount Pictures now has the rights to the Republic properties.

With the rights to many old films falling into public domain, other companies have brought out edited and remixed versions of our favorite films. John Wayne was brought to color by Word Productions in a series of "Young Duke Films" complete with new soundtracks. Malofilm restored, reedited, and distributed many popular cowboy classics in the early 1990s. Front Row Entertainment and Good Times Video have distributed classics for over a decade and continues to dig deep into the vaults and reintroduce westerns to a new generation.

Today, the sources of western films and television shows are many. Big box discount retailers, large entertainment stores, Wal-Mart, and Walgreens carry a good supply of western films. Online retailers such as Amazon, eBay (new and used), the museums (Roy Rogers, Rex Allen, Gene Autry Heritage), and dedicated movie retailers such as Westerns.com, Movies Unlimited, and Comet Video can usually supply your want list.

www.amazon.com

www.eBay.com

www.royrogers.com
(Roy Rogers episodes, movies and
    productions)

www.pinkbanana.com/rex
(Rex Allen episodes and movies)

www.westerns.com

www.moviesunlimited.com

Comet Video
PO Box 750
Franklin NC 28744-0750
828-524-5251
http://www.peedeeworld.net/~co
    metvideo/home.htm

www.ccvideo.com

www.rareserials.com
Jim's Rare Serials & B Westerns
PO Box 477

Rt 422E
Penn Run PA 15765
724-349-4455
(PAL and NTSC videos available)

Bill Sasser, convention organizer extraordinaire, has had the opportunity over the years of meeting the best of the west. Through his efforts, we are able to share in the panel discussions of years past. Panel discussion guests include William Witney, Rex Allen, Rex Allen Jr., Peggy Stewart, Lash LaRue, Chief Thundercloud and many, many more. You can order video tapes from him at

Bill Sasser
PO Box 524
Gloucester Pt VA 23063
804-642-5858

Episode guides are a video lover's best friend. Most popular TV shows have, at some point, had some episode guide produced by an ardent fan. There are several listed in Chapter 5, and many more available that were not listed. Episode guides typically list cast, credits, plot summaries, air dates, and re-run dates, and include photographs or other related information. To purchase the guide to your favorite show, try www.amazon.com, or www.eBay.com. Episode information is also available online. Here are four sources to try:

www.TVland.com
(A general overview of each show with some episodes listed)

www.geocities.com/TampaChatr/index.html
(Cast listings and histories for major productions)

www.tvtome.com

www.yesterdayland.com
(Show histories and cast listings)

Dedicated Web sites will often include an episode list or a link to one. Search for your favorite show and hunt for the episode list; it's worth the time. If you are looking for productions with particular actors, one good source is the Internet Movie Database (www.imdb.com), which includes movie appearances, television appearances, production credits, and links to pertinent pages. It is the most reliable source for online information. You can also try searching the name of an actor or actress on Amazon (www.amazon.com), though it usually lists acting roles only, and is more of a retail portal.

Davy Crockett album from Walt Disney.

Music and Folios

As many of the western stars were singing cowboys, there are substantial numbers of recordings available. Gene Autry was popular as a recording artist prior to his film career, as were Rex Allen, Roy Rogers, Dale Evans (radio), Jimmy Wakely and Tex Ritter. After their film careers were over, many stars returned to the concert stage or recording studio and performed until retirement or death. Stars like Rex Allen, Roy Rogers, Tex Ritter, and Jimmy Wakely experienced even greater success after their film and television careers and as a result have been recognized for contributions to both the film and recording industries.

At one time it was common for studios to release soundtrack albums for popular western movies, but those albums are now hard to find. No longer can you get the entire soundtrack to *Oh Susanna*, instead you might find the title track and, if you are lucky, one more recording on a "best of" collection. Compilation albums are the most common, with the bulk of early recordings now lost. For the major artists, more effort has been made to restore and remaster the existing recordings to be more acceptable to

Gene Autry compilations, 1992 releases.

Roy Rogers CDs: *Tribute* (1991), *Best of* (1990).

today's listeners. Collectors still possess copies of original recordings such as "Silver Haired Daddy of Mine" by Gene Autry. The less familiar songs, though no less entertaining, are now missing or incomplete. However, 78s, 33s, CDs, and sometimes concert videos of your favorite stars are available from various collectors and online dealers.

Eric Von Hamersveld, author of *It Was Always the Music*, in the course of his research has discovered a disturbing fact. Original recordings of the movie music that we love do not exist. The music is on the soundtracks, of course, but as noted in Chapter 8, the films and the soundtracks we would love to restore are badly damaged already, or destroyed. The studios are not a reliable source for original recordings, unless some forward-thinking individual saved them from the trash bin. The stars themselves usually do not possess original recordings, unless they purchased a print of the film from the studio. The best we can do is to take existing recordings and remaster the music. As a result, the present reissues do not necessarily reflect the original recordings, though in some cases they are superior in video and audio quality.

Recording catalogues and discographies (listing of recordings) for most artists are available, and can provide useful information for the collector seeking to complete a collection of an artist's life work. Sources for recording artists discographies and recordings include:

www.CDnow.com   www.purecountrymusic.com

www.recordmaster.com   www.artistdirect.com

Recordings, like books and comics, are coded for identification. Each disk is labeled with the following information:

> Writer
> Singer
> Record label
> Release code
> Accompaniment
> Source (e.g., "from *Oh, Susanna*")
> Producer

To find out more about historical recordings, look for the *Official Price Guide to Records*, which can be found at your local bookstore.

Folios and sheet music are a real treat for the collector. Sheet music usually includes a piano and vocal score for a popular song; a folio is a collection of sheet music, usually with a specific theme. Roy Rogers, Gene Autry and the other singing western stars were the subject of folios. Sheet music was also sold, much as it is now, for specific songs, and is quite rare in good condition.

Pricing information is listed in sheet music price guides, and often in the character guides as well.

Amazon, eBay, estate sales, and auction houses are good sources for collectible recordings and folios.

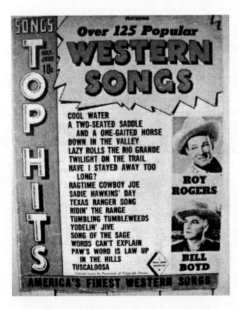

1940s popular Western songs folio.			1940s *On the Old Spanish Trail* folio.

Compact discs are found on the net at:

www.amazon.com

www.westerns.com

www.rhinorecords.com
(Retro releases and classic albums)

www.purecountry.com

www.cduniverse.com

www.artistdirect.com
(Biography, albums, song downloads)

You can't keep a good record down!

Radio Comedy and Drama

Radio dramas are like TV without pictures, only better. With a good sound effects crew, good scripting, and a listener with a good imagination, radio dramas bring space, the west, or your favorite comedies to life in sparkling color.

For almost 25 years, radio presentations were the preferred family entertainment. Family members of all ages gathered around the RCA in anticipation of the evening's offerings.

Many characters made the jump from radio to television, the comics pages, or the movies. *Blondie, The Shadow, The Lone Ranger, Captain Midnight, The Green Hornet, Gunsmoke, Have Gun Will Travel,* and many other shows made successful transitions. Some of the popular characters appeared in all four media at the same time!

Today, with the advent of affordable digital technology and recordable CDs, it is possible to purchase compact discs with over 600 radio shows. With digital technology, the static and drop that characterizes analog recordings can be eliminated and signals can be enhanced. Purists prefer the "feel" of the original, while newer audiences prefer the cleaner, digital versions.

The Lone Ranger Chronicles tape set.

Analog tape at its best was able to hold only 120 minutes of audio, and reel-to-reel length determined the running time of the recordings. MP3 recordings can run over 100 hours. The MP3 format is truly a blessing for the "Episodologist."

We have been fortunate to have collectors who preserved radio drama through the decades. From their efforts, we are able to enjoy *Fibber McGee and Molly*, *The Shadow*, *Roy Rogers*, *The Lone Ranger*, and many more classic shows.

Early radio drama was broadcast live and not recorded. It is only since the mid 1930s that the scripts have been recorded and saved for archival considerations. Dedicated professionals have allowed us to peek into the past, when life was simpler.

Dedicated episode guides for the classic shows are rare, but they can be found. Jim Harmon, a collector, dealer and scholar, has written *Those Great Radio Heroes*, and many more radio drama treatises. Terry Salomonson has produced radio log books on comedies (*The Great Gildersleeve*, *Lum 'n' Abner*), adventure series (*Dragnet*, *Green Hornet*, *The Lone Ranger*, *Challenge of the Yukon*, *Yours Truly Johnny Dollar*), and science fiction that represent thousands of hours of research and joy. He can be contacted at

> Terry Salomonson
> Radio Classics
> PO Box 347
> Howell MI 48844-0347

For the dedicated radio drama fan, SPERDVAC (Society for Preservation and Encouragement of Radio Drama, Variety and Comedy) can be found on the Web at www.sperdvac.org.

Additionally, Jerry Haendiges maintains a wonderful Web site, "Jerry's Vintage Radio Logs," at www.otrsite.com.

Another interesting old time radio Web site is www.old-time.com. This Web site contains excellent information on the programs, culture and premiums associated with the classic radio shows.

Episodes of great radio drama can be found for sale on the Internet at www.eBay.com and www.amazon.com.

Weekly radio dramas are presented via the Internet at www.cowboy-pal.com.

Jim Harmon maintains an extensive list of radio episodes and movie serials for sale and can be contacted at:

> Jim Harmon
> 634 S Orchard Dr
> Burbank CA 91506

The number of old time radio dealers is growing. Go to your favorite search engine and check out what you find. You'll be glad you did.

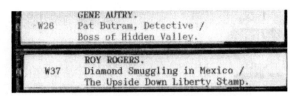

| W28 | GENE AUTRY.
Pat Butram, Detective /
Boss of Hidden Valley. |
| W37 | ROY ROGERS.
Diamond Smuggling in Mexico /
The Upside Down Liberty Stamp. |

Roy Rogers and Gene Autry radio plays.

Can you hear that static? Is it time for *The Lone Ranger* already?

Premiums

Wow! The toys they used to give away!

From 1928 on, radio advertisers used premiums to promote their products and to gauge the popularity of a program. The first Lone Ranger giveaway in 1933 produced a huge response that amazed WXYZ and George Trendle. Many more premiums quickly followed.

Premiums include such items as rings, forts, guns, cups, cookbooks, badges, masks, and pins. The listener could redeem points or box tops or just send his address to receive the jewel of the day. Ralston sponsored Tom Mix; General Mills pushed the Lone Ranger on cereal boxes; and Quaker Oats fed the Gabby Hayes–Roy Rogers frenzy.

Recently, General Mills (Cheerios) released a retro Lone Ranger commemorative lunch kit and cereal box in the United States that became an instant collector's item.

Popular western character premiums include the Cisco Kid, the cast of *Death Valley Days*, Frank Buck, Gabby Hayes, the Lone Ranger, Lone Wolf, Red Ryder, Roy Rogers, Sgt. Preston, Straight Arrow, and Tom Mix.

The values of radio premiums range from a few dollars to several hundred. The Lone Ranger Frontier Town is one of the most sought-after sets,

Lone Ranger cereal box and lunch kit.

Rare near complete Cheerios Frontier Town.

and consequently fetches $500 or more in auctions. Other rare premiums include the Cisco Kid Cattle Brand Kit, the Lone Ranger Secret Compartment Ring, Sgt. Preston 10 in 1 Trail Kit, and the Tom Mix decoder six-gun.

For a complete listing of radio premium values, consult the *Official Hake's Price Guide to Character Toys*, Jim Harmon's *Radio and TV Premiums*, www.old-time.com/premiums or www.kovels.com.

Afterword

The collectibles field is huge. This book is meant to be a primer, to lead you to the place where you can acquire more knowledge in your chosen field of collecting. Buy the recommended books (see Chapter 5), and check out new editions as they are printed. Read magazines; search the Internet; go to swap meets, auctions, or shows. There is no substitute for personal experience.

Most of all: Have fun! These are toys we are talking about, aren't they? Hmmm...

7

Trading Posts: Buying, Selling and Swapping

After reading the last chapter, you should have an idea where your interests lie, and where to find more information on either the collectibles themselves or the hobby you are engrossed in.

In the last few years, with the advent and explosion of the Internet and its limitless resources, access to world marketplaces is now as close as your computer. Prior to the computerization of the collectible market, only a fortunate few had access to the conventions and the dealers that gave birth to the industry.

But there is still a lot to learn. Where and what should you buy? How do you sell and ship items? How do you handle the payment process? Is it possible to trade items with other collectors? Here are some tips.

Buying

The number of collectibles dealers is vast; it would be impossible to list them all. Here, I will list some companies, often recognized as prominent, reputable, and stable. (NOTE: This does not constitute an endorsement for any of the listed companies. They are simply suggested as companies likely to satisfy your orders.)

The most prominent Web site sources for collectibles are, without a doubt, www.amazon.com and www.eBay.com. Both Web sites offer collectibles of every sort imaginable. Autographs, books, comics, dolls, figurines, guitars, guns, holsters, Indians, cookie jars, knives, letters, manuscripts, cards, puzzles, portfolios, Roy Rogers items, six-guns, underwear, Zorro items, and much, much more can all be found in all price ranges.

EBay and Amazon can both list by category, price range, and type of item. Both Web sites allow you to purchase new or used items. Both Web sites offer payment and shipping options directly accessible from their Web site. Both also offer conflict resolution, insurance, and "retail" shops.

EBay has introduced several options that allow the user to access new items as well as "used." You can see auctions and check out the first price, last price, highest price, or lowest price. You can search descriptions for content (titles are not always accurate). Half.com, eBay Motors, and eBay Stores are all options that give the buyer and seller customization on their transaction types.

EBay offers payment options for the users that allow easy online transactions via credit card, U.S. bank account, or regular mail. With eBay's recent acquisition of Paypal, purchases are more automated and can be done with a click of your mouse. Shipping can also be arranged online as well to make your transaction smooth and trouble free. Buyer and seller ratings are provided to give you an idea of who you are dealing with and their history with transactions. On "My eBay," you as a buyer can monitor auctions you have bid on, auctions you are winning, auctions you are hosting, your feedback rating, your profile, and a "remind me" service for pre-set searches.

Amazon offers similar services, except for layout. Their home page has a tab type design that allows you to specify which type of item you want to search for. Books, popular music, magazines, subscriptions, music downloads, classical music, DVDs, VHS, restaurants, movie show times, baby items, toys, computers, video games, electronics, auctions, and cars are some of the categories that are available for searching. In terms of payment options, you can purchase online via credit card, U.S. bank accounts, and regular mail. You can arrange shipping online. You can access your account, as on eBay, and view the balance if you choose to do so. Commissions can be earned on affiliate programs and deposited to your account, and then used to purchase items at a discount. With searches, results are sorted down the center column, other related items (including your rating of the item) are listed to the left, and the right column serves as a "list" suggestion. Book searches yield reviews, publisher, ISBN, pages, related books, related authors, and the ability to add the book to your shopping cart. Most items follow this format.

EBay was designed as a means to sell unwanted items through Internet auctions, while Amazon was originally an online bookstore. Both have evolved into full-service buy-and-sell hubs, with loyal dedicated customer bases. Each is useful for different purposes. Amazon offers more "editorial review" content from the publisher or manufacturer, while eBay offers the more casual approach.

Either way, type in "Roy Rogers" and be prepared to spend time in front of your monitor. Guard your wallet, though: The temptation may be too much.

Another good source for collectible items is Heritage Comics, who can be found on the Internet at www.heritagecomics.com. Heritage Comics is also part of a larger group that deals in coins and stamps. For the last couple of years, the comics site has offered platinum to silver age comics, original artwork, and related memorabilia in auction on either a monthly or a quarterly basis. Key issues and items have gone for record amounts in recent auctions, with several copies of *Action* 1, *Batman* 1, and *Superman* 1 being sold.

An excellent dedicated toy and memorabilia auction house since 1967, Hake's Collectibles has a long history of terrific items that have been sold. Ted Hake, author of the *Official Hake's Price Guide to Character Toys*, is extremely active in this field and is regarded as an expert. His monthly auction features western items, radio items, premiums, election memorabilia, and much more for the hard-to-please collector. Hakes offers consignment services and also maintains an active "want list" for both his collection and yours. Printed catalogues are available. He can be reached at

> www.hakes.com
> Hake's Americana & Collectibles
> PO Box 1444
> York PA 17405
> 717-848-1333

Sotheby's is perhaps the best known auction house in the world. Serving also as a highly respected appraisal center, Sotheby's has set the mark for the collectibles industry. Sellers of comic books, furniture, well known estates, artwork, coins, and any item of appreciable value, they can be contacted at

> www.sothebys.com
> Sotheby's
> 1334 York Ave
> New York NY 10021
> 212-606-7000

The following Web sites are good sources of western star memorabilia:

> www.royrogers.com
> (Roy Rogers' home page)

> www.pinkbanana.com/rex
> (Rex Allen's home page)

> www.autry-museum.org
> (Gene Autry Western Heritage Museum's home page)

www.cowboypal.com
(A good "heads up" site on western memorabilia)

http://members.tripod.com/~ClaytonMoore
(Steve Jensen has compiled this great Lone Ranger site, packed
with useful links to interviews, articles, and the Lone Ranger
news including upcoming products. You can't go wrong here.)

Garage Sales, Flea Markets, Estate Sales

Garage sales, flea markets, and local estate sales and auctions are a
great place to find treasures. Odds are, the person selling the item does
not have a personal interest in the gems you are after. As a result, you can
get some pretty good deals right in your own back yard.

Some things to note, though: check the items thoroughly for completeness, marks, and cracks. Even though a Breyer may cost you only a
quarter, you may as well get a good one.

Ask if they have any more. You never know if there is a box that didn't
make the garage sale, just full of great western items you'd love to take off
their hands.

Get to the garage sale or flea market early if they are advertising western collectibles. Some other keen soul may beat you to the treasures of the
show if you arrive late.

Check the boxes thoroughly. Estate sales often yield a real gem that
is tucked in the bottom of a box or shelf. Bid on the last few items. A box
may yield enough profit for you to purchase a substantial item from somewhere else.

Know what you are looking for, and what you are willing to pay. You
don't want to overspend your budget, and there is nothing worse than
overlooking the item that could complete your collection (or be a great
swap for someone else).

Antique Stores

Antique stores or malls can be a source of great cowboy collectibles
or great disappointment.

Although the supply of western collectibles is drying up as it is
directed to eBay, Amazon, or high profile auctions, local stores will often
still have stocks of western related merchandise. As with garage sales, you
have to know what you are looking for, and what you are willing to spend
on particular items.

Prices may seem high in stores, but that doesn't mean the stores are trying to gouge you. Online auctions such as eBay have conditioned us to low prices that do not always reflect an item's true value. A copy of *Dale Evans and the River of Peril* may sell for $5 on eBay (not including $7.50 shipping and handling) and $20 at an antique store, but $20 may be closer to the real value. It may be that the store paid $10 for the book and needs $10 more to stay open. An advantage of buying at a store is that you do not have to wait for the item to be shipped.

Antique malls are a great way to spend a couple of hours. As many as one hundred stores may combine to form a mall. For the buyer, the selection of items available is a godsend, and sometimes results in a trip well spent.

Antique shows are also a good location for treasure hunting. Dealers who attend these shows will often bring only their best items. The hunter may come away delighted or disappointed, but that's all part of the hunt.

Want Lists

If you collect a specific character or type of memorabilia, shopping by a want list is an option. Several dealers will maintain an active list of customer wants, and when an item shows up, they call the appropriate customer. Other online dealers will email the customer when the item is in their inventory. Some will hunt for the item, rather than waiting for it to come along.

Want lists take the work out of collecting. You do not have to do the legwork; no need to search through lists, catalogues and databases. Many dealers who utilize want lists use the same sources that this book recommends.

The hunt is sometimes more exciting than the purchase. If you enjoy the chase, a want list may not be for you. But if you are too busy to take the time to surf and scan, then the want list may be the way to go.

EBay and Amazon both have services that will alert you when an item matching what you want comes up.

Purchasing Options

Today, there are several options when it comes to paying for items. You can pay via money orders, personal checks, electronic checks, credit cards, cash, and online payment systems.

Money orders and personal checks often create the most banking havoc. For a customer from Canada purchasing an item from the United States (or vice versa) banking fees can be as high as $10. Additionally, when dealing with checks, there is a clearing period of as much as two weeks. Even before shipping, a transaction can take up to five weeks before payment has been finalized this way.

Cash sent through the mail is one way to avoid bank fees, even though banks will discount the exchange rate. Cash sent through the mail should be sent wrapped in brown paper for security reasons. The postal service discourages sending cash through the mail. If it is lost it cannot be reimbursed.

Electronic checking accounts and electronic money transfers are very efficient. There are a variety of electronic methods by which money can be transferred. Paypal, Billpoint, and Electronic Gold accounts (eGold) can be used to transfer funds from account to account, and every step is secure, traceable and verifiable. Best of all, there are no banking fees to convert currencies over the Internet. Fees are incurred only when the receiver transfers funds to other accounts or onto a credit card.

Some dealers will not use electronic transactions, but rather will have you email your credit card number in a variety of ways. You can email the sixteen digit number, expiration date, and security code in separate emails. Or you can email the entire number set in one email.

Telephone credit card sales can also be done. The credit card user can give the seller his or her card numbers over the phone. If there is trust with the person, this can work well.

Every individual has a comfort zone. Some comfort zones include the use of Internet transfers, and some do not. Find yours and stick to it.

Shipping, Handling and Customs

In today's world of Internet transactions, the real winners are the shipping companies. FedEx, UPS, and Purolator Courier have all benefited from online shopping. It's one thing to buy the item, but another to get it there.

After an online purchase is made, you usually have to include shipping and handling charges. Sometimes these charges far exceed the cost of the item. Most Web sites with a shopping cart system will enable you to choose the desired shipping method and will calculate it into the total. Others will calculate the U.S. shipping charges, and then will email you the correct invoice amount back.

When items cross the border, the customs and duties officers (CCRA in Canada, and Customs in the U.S.) inspect the declaration form to verify the item is what it says. In the case of Canada, a $5 fee may be charged, and a tax of 7 percent (GST) is also added in. If the item is declared a gift, there should be no charge from customs. When goods are shipped from Canada to the States, duties and levies are also charged to the item. As a rule of thumb, when a Canadian purchases from the States, double the cost of the item and add $5.

Canadians also have to consider the variable exchange rate. An item purchased for $10 U.S. is $16 CDN (currently). Add shipping and handling of $10 U.S., $5 customs and $1 CDN tax, and the total cost is now $38 CDN!

Valuation

The value that you place on your collection will always be more than what others place on it. This is an absolute, incontrovertible fact.

Collectibles have many values. Market value, book value, sentimental value, and historical value are only four. We value our own collections in terms of sentimental value. Buyers value collections in terms of book value. Historians value collections in terms of historical significance. Dealers value collections in terms of market value. At any given time, we as collectors can be any or all of these.

The market value of an item is the price that a buyer is willing to pay or the market is able to bear.

The book value is the average price that others have paid for similar or identical collectibles in similar condition over a period of time. Book values are derived from price guides. If the price guide lists your Roy Rogers Hartland figure at $20, it may sell for that, or it may sell for $40. You never know which price is accurate until you sell.

The sentimental value of an item cannot be fairly gauged. For someone who has met Clayton Moore and been given a silver bullet or an old hat, the item is priceless. For the collector, a ballpark number may be placed on the item. No matter what price is obtained or deemed to be "accurate," it will never be enough for the awestruck fan.

Historical value is not monetary and is therefore more difficult to pin down. The monetary value of an authentic Buffalo Bill vest may be in the thousands, but in terms of history, it is almost priceless, and truly irreplaceable.

For insurance and listing purposes, book value is an accepted standard.

Many collectors find it useful to keep records of the items in their collections, noting their value. As a suggestion, I offer the following format for listing collectibles:

Character	Lone Ranger/ Clayton Moore
Type of Collectible	Sunglasses Stand, Rare
Production Date	1980s when mask was taken
Condition	Good image
Value	$15 (?)
Notes	Holes punched in cardboard, writing on image

A listing of this style has a couple of advantages. You have a picture of your collectible for insurance purposes if losses occur, and it makes an attractive sales presentation if people are interested in buying. It is also versatile enough to be used for many types of items.

For comic books and books, I suggest the following format:

Title	Pub.	Number	Year	Cond.	Value	Notes
Batman	DC	21	1944	G/VG	$225	Cowboy cover

For movies, I have used a similar style with different headings:

Tape #	Actor	Title	Speed	Start	Stop	Value	Genre
621	Roy Rogers	Son of Paleface	SP	0:00	2:00	$19.95	West

For hardcover and paperbacks, again, similar style with different headings:

Author	Pub	Title	Number	Cond	Value	Notes	Yr/Cpyrt
William Turner	Medallion	Gunpoint	Y976	Good	$2	Inside markings	Sept, 1964

You can also use the same format as the Long Ranger sunglasses stand example (vertical categories and entries) for these listings. You can also include a photograph for ease of identification. Different collectibles have variant covers, making photographs a useful tool in differentiating editions and prints.

With different databases like Excel, the collector can develop different records for various types of collectibles. You can also add columns up to provide a total value for your collection.

Prewritten software exists for the listing and valuation of your collectibles.

Selling Strategies

When the time comes for you to part with some of your beloved toys and collectibles, there are many points to consider.

Prior to selling collectibles, make a list of what you have to sell. (If you have already done so, you are more organized than 90 percent of collectors.) The previous section should give you a good basis for developing your list.

Listing of collectibles should include:

Character
Manufacturer
Detailed description of item
Year of production (if known)
Condition of item using industry standards
Photograph (if possible)
Approximate value (according to marketplace or catalogue)

Different strategies exist for the sale of collectibles. Some are labor intensive, while others require minimal effort.

EBay and Amazon are two good destinations for collectible auctions. They offer the chance to include a photograph of your item, and the added convenience of electronic banking and shipping.

The real work comes in when you have to list each item accurately, check for copyright or trademark infringement (now a concern), find a photograph host, decide on auction options (feature, double listing, gift icon) and decide what kind of auction you want to have. You can have a reserve auction, where a certain bid has to be met before the item is considered sold. You can host a no-reserve auction, where the high bid wins. You can host a private auction, where invited bidders compete for the item. Another option is "Buy It Now," where the item can be purchased for a fixed price above the opening bid.

Every auction type has its pitfalls. Reserve auctions usually do not finish successfully. Private auctions are not successful unless you have motivated buyers. Regular auctions frequently finish with low sale prices, which translates into less than what you expected. There can be bidding frenzies, driving prices up, or few bidders, keeping the price down. "Buy It Now" auctions seem to work best for collectibles of real value.

You really have to consider your options carefully. This is, after all, your collection. And the real work is just beginning. There is waiting for the payment, packing the item, shipping it out, and finally, saying good-bye to your favorite things.

A more attractive option is consigning your collectibles to an established auction house. You send the items to the auction house; they sell them and give you the money, keeping a percentage for themselves. The established auction houses hold regular auctions, advertise effectively, and have a large client base that ensures the best money for your items. Hake's Memorabilia, Heritage Auctions, Sotheby's Auctions, and High Noon Auctions all serve as consignment houses. A buyer's premium of 10–15 percent is applied to the final sale price to pay the auction house for its efforts.

Prior to sending your items, you must make a list of the proposed items and forward it to the house. Depending on the items, swaps or advances can be obtained. Each dealer has different guidelines. The better houses can be found at

www.sothebys.com
Sotheby's
1334 York Ave
New York NY 10021
212-606-7000

www.hakes.com
Hake's Americana & Collectibles
PO Box 1444
York PA 17405
717-848-1333

www.heritagecomics.com
100 Highland Park Village
Second Fl
Dallas TX 75205
800-872-6467

www.highnoon.com
High Noon Auctions
9929 Venice Blvd
Los Angeles CA 90034
310-202-9010

www.mastronet.com
Mastro Net Inc
1515 W 22nd St
Ste 125
Oak Brook IL 60523
630-472-1200

Local antique stores may also take consignment or swap items. However, unless you live in a high traffic area, results may be slow and somewhat less than you expect.

Another common option is selling the items yourself on your own Web site. You already have your items listed, and perhaps photographed. The most difficult step is to design (or have designed for you) a Web site to feature your items. Web site hosting can be free at select sites, but if you pay to have an antique store online, then the hosting is included. An element too often forgotten in Web site design is updating with new links, content, and format changes when necessary. This process is labor intensive, and impractical unless you are Web-savvy and have the resources and time to invest into your Web site.

Selling your items to an established dealer is the most painful option. Having done so on different occasions, I can attest that the separation anxiety is almost numbing. Some general rules of thumb follow:

1. Be prepared with a detailed list and approximate value.
2. Be prepared with a low end figure that you will accept.
3. Be prepared to walk away. Dealers frequently pay less than 40 percent of the value or retail price unless you have a really hot item.
4. Be mindful of your low end limit.
5. Deal for the package, not just for the pristine items. Many dealers will

take lower quality and valued items just to get the gem of the collection.

6. Be prepared to be disappointed.
7. Take trades to increase the value of your return. Dealers will more likely trade than buy. Remember, the dealer is in business to make a profit. You are selling because you need either money or space.
8. Contact your friendly dealers first. You are more likely to get a fair price.
9. Research your proposed buyers. Be certain the dealer has an interest in your type of collectible, or has customers who do.
10. If you are selling to an Internet dealer, clarify shipping and pricing issues before you send any items.

Most importantly of all, be certain you are ready to sell. You may have invested many hours searching and hunting for the book you just sold for $5. Seller's remorse can be worse than buyer's remorse!

Garage sales may be a means to sell your items. One great drawback is the issue of "bargain bin" pricing. Most garage sale shoppers expect bargains, unless the buyer is a collector and is aware of your item's value (which can be worse sometimes). Some guidelines follow:

1. Do not haggle just to take a loss and sell your items. You will be disappointed in your take.
2. In advertising your sale, listing "Collectible books and comics, Roy Rogers toys," and so on can greatly increase traffic.
3. As in the case of selling to dealers, be prepared to take a loss, and to have a hard time saying goodbye.
4. Delicate items should be labeled as such. A damaged comic book devalues very quickly.
5. Mark prices clearly, in more than one spot.
6. Have fun, and share your enthusiasm for your hobby.

Garage sales can also backfire. There is always one person that walks up and says "Say, do you want more of those? I have a box of...." Goodbye to your profits! Hello to more goodies!

You can list your collectibles in the newspaper under antiques or an appropriate section, on a free listing Web site, or in a collectors' magazine or Web page. A sample ad might read:

> For Sale: Complete Roy Rogers comic book collection, Roy Rogers toys, Roy Rogers clothes, Hopalong Cassidy blanket, Lone Ranger books. Will swap for new computer. No reasonable offer refused. Call Tim at xxx-xxxxx for more information.

Or

You may strike paydirt and be able to sell your items for a good price. Key items have been sold for high dollar amounts, or swapped for houses and cars! You may not be that lucky. Collectibles work that way. They have value only for the right person.

Swaps and Trades

All collectors manage to find doubles or even triples of items. And all collectors talk about their beloved books, cards, pictures, movies, costumes and whatever they have among themselves.

This invariably leads to the topic of trades.

Trades can be good or bad. A good trade is one in which both parties obtain something they want. A bad trade is when one does, and one doesn't.

Swaps and trades, in terms of payment, are usually far more equitable than selling. You and your trading partner set the parameters and conditions, then swap. Instead of getting $5 for a $20 hardcover, you may get $25 worth of comic books.

Trades can be fun. Two Lone Ranger hardcovers and a comic for a Roy Rogers guitar. Three Breyer figures (with missing hands) for a complete Johnny West and Thunderbolt. My kingdom for a horse! And the list can go on.

Like a baseball team, you can trade for future considerations and the first Roy Rogers standee that comes in. Or you can trade with dealers for items and a little extra cash.

It all happens, and it is always a learning experience.

When you do trade, be careful to verify the exchange (if done via regular mail), and to offer the ability to re-swap if the other party is not satisfied. If you swap with a friend, make sure both of you are happy. There is nothing worse than hurting a friendship over a mere collectible!

8

Though Decay May Call: Care and Preservation Techniques

"Once upon a time, when I was a kid, I had them all: Roy Rogers, Batman, Superman, Gene Autry, the Lone Ranger. And I saved them. After my friends and I had read the issue, I put it in a box in the corner of my room. When I left for college, my mom put them in the basement, and they got wet one spring. I came home to visit, and threw them all out..."

Or:

"I had those pistols when I was a kid. Used to take them everywhere, to school, to church, to bed. One day, the handles broke, and mom took the pistols when I was sleeping and tossed them in the garbage. Boy, I loved those pistols..."

Or:

"Mice..."

"Sunbleached..."

"Donated..."

"All bent out of shape..."

"Complete, except for one piece..."

We have all heard these stories, and we all have at least one that we tell about, the "one that got away," or the "box Uncle Ted was supposed to give me." They make great conversation and convey a great warning too.

As seasoned (or soon to be wise) collectors, we have to be very careful with our collectibles. Many of us have spent countless hours chasing and hunting until we actually could call that treasure ours. Now that we have it, what do we do? Time can be our worst enemy, or our greatest ally, depending on whether we take the appropriate steps to preserve and protect.

Let us now consider the various elements that lead to the eventual decay of our collectibles. The main elements are moisture, temperature, pH, composition, amount of direct sunlight, atmospheric pollution, original condition, protection style and storage method.

Moisture: The more humid an environment, the more likely that mold and decay will set in. The ideal percentage of humidity varies somewhat for each type of item, but it is usually in the neighborhood of 50 percent.

Temperature: Temperature can speed up or slow down decay of collectibles. The higher the temperature in a storage environment, the more brittle an item gets (as moisture content decreases), and the more quickly chemical processes lead to decay or discoloration and increased flammability. Generally speaking, 68 degrees Fahrenheit is the standard.

pH: The pH of an item is important as well. For long term storage and preservation, the pH should be in the neutral range (6–8), with the ideal being 7.0. If an item is too acidic or basic, chemical decomposition will occur. Colors may change, the surfaces may become brittle, or there may be an odor associated with the item.

Composition: The composition of an item directly affects the type of preservation that you do, and the urgency with which you do it. If you collect pulp magazines, comic books, comic strips, promotional material, articles, or any paper item, you will have to contend with high risk due to high pH. Pulp based items deteriorate quickly if stored in high humidity and temperature. If you collect plastic items, be aware that some older plastics contain oils that turn yellow with age or exposure to the sun. Some items (e.g., Egyptian artifacts, nitrate films), when exposed to normal air and light conditions, deteriorate rapidly.

Direct sunlight: Exposure to direct sunlight is not recommended. There is a reported case of one collector who had stored his *Batman* 1–10 originals in his bedroom in direct sunlight. The colors faded within a couple of years, and consequently rendered his very rare issues almost worthless. Pictures, newsprint, clothing, or anything with pigment fades in direct sunlight. Indirect lighting methods are recommended.

Atmospheric pollution: Especially important to paper goods, the sulfur dioxide turns paper yellow with time. Garage storage is not recommended.

Original condition: Probably the largest factor in the amount of deterioration is the original condition of the item. If you have a perfect copy of *Batman* 125, the amount of loss you can expect is less as you have more to work with. If the condition is already low, with no cover gloss and high pH, then the amount of deterioration will be high unless you can neutralize the pH. The better the original condition, the longer the item will last in reasonable condition.

Storage methods: Every type of collectible has a recommended method of storage. If the item is exposed to undue stress and strain, then damage will occur. Some items, such as albums, video tapes, DVDs, comic books, books, and toys, should be stored vertically. Other items can be stored horizontally.

Protection style: Acid free sprays, neutralizing sprays and solutions, newer staples, acid free bags, and other strategies all have their place. Many advertised methods do not work, and sometimes you have to pay the premium for protection from decay.

Paper and Pulp Goods

The storage of pulp-based collectibles such as comic books, paper-backs, and magazines is tricky. Generally speaking, these types of items should be stored in an upright position (or flat with no weight on them), in an acid free protective bag, and the collectible should be pH neutral. The temperature, humidity, and light conditions should also be standard (40–50 percent humidity, 68 degrees Fahrenheit, indirect lighting).

For comic books, magazines and paperbacks, there should also be an acid free backing board to provide firmness for the spines. These come in all sizes and shapes. Mylar products are recognized as the best in this area. Polypropylene and polypropylethene protective bags serve well for a few years, but should be changed after five years to a Mylar product as the chemicals break down and the bag and stored item yellow slightly.

If you have more items than can comfortably be stored on a bookshelf, it is best to store them in special acid free boxes made for storing comics, books and magazines. The ends should be "insulated" with an acid free board to protect the first and last items from moisture and chemicals.

Then there is the "I lost my collection to a flood" scenario, which leads us to the best possible advice: *Store your items above the ground*, on shelves, lest the evil moisture creep into your treasures and render them mildew traps. Do not store your books against an outside wall, as condensation can also affect your collectibles. A reasonable air flow should be maintained.

One of the best sources of acid free supplies is:

> Bill Cole Enterprises
> PO Box 60
> Randolph MA 02368-0060
> 781-986-2653
> www.bcemylar.com

They have a complete selection for acid free, Mylar and archival supplies for any collectible.

If you have a paper collectible that has been damaged by time, help is available. There are companies that can restore your paper collectible. Possible services include whitening, flattening, cleaning, tape removal, piece replacement, tear repair, deacidification, color retouching, staple replacement, and spine roll removal. Books that are restored generally rise in value, but are noted as restored in any auction or valuation.

Here is some contact information for a few restorers:

Fantasy Masterpieces
PO Box 881
Kelso WA 98626
360-577-0351

Classic Conservations
PO Box 2335
Slidell LA 70459
504-639-0621

Renaissance Restoration Lab
81 Riverwood Parkway
Toronto, Ontario
Canada
M8Y 4E4
416-231-1272
birkemoe@interlog.com

The Restoration Lab
29 Angela Ln
Watertown MA 02472
617-9241-4297

Another advocate of proper archival storage is the CGC or Comics Guarantee Group. Primarily a company to certify comic books in an impartial professional manner, this group has another function: to protect collectibles from the ravages of time. Their services include comic book grading, certification, and preservation in a high impact, tamper proof airtight folder. A CGC grade is an industry recognized standard that adds liquidity to an investment. They can be contacted at:

Comics Guarantee Group
PO Box 4738
Sarasota FL 34230
877-NMCOMIC
941-360-3991
www.cgccomics.com

TRADING CARDS

Trading cards come in all shapes and sizes. The standard size, as most cards are now, is 2½" × 3½". Early trading cards were larger, usually 3" × 5" (nickelodeon cards). The British Roy Rogers cards were even smaller.

As trading cards are primarily a pulp product, collectors should use the same strategies that preserve comics, books, and magazines. Fortunately, just as the comic book industry changed its printing paper during the 1980s, collectors' cards, too, are now printed on glossier, heavier, more expensive and relatively low-acid stock. Modern printing variations include gold signatures, foil imprints, holographic images, and special inserts.

Trading cards should be kept in acid free card sheets or sleeves. Protective sleeves can hold one card or 18 (depending on the layout). Sleeves can be free standing and sealed, or loose and made of cheap plastic. Collector-grade card sheets can protect the card from pH changes, the cover gloss from being removed, and the card corners from being compromised. Various sizes of protector sheets are available.

Card protector supplies can be purchased from sports cards shops. Other good sources are

> Bill Cole Enterprises
> PO Box 60
> Randolph MA 02368-0060
> 781-986-2653
> www.bcemylar.com
>
> www.warp9cards.com
> (modern cards and supplies)

MOVIE POSTERS AND LOBBY CARDS

The protection of lobby cards and movie posters is primarily the same as for other paper goods. The standard conditions apply for humidity, temperature, pH, and light placement.

There are, however, some important differences. Some lobby cards ("lobbies") measure 8½" × 11", like most comic books, but more often they are 11" × 14". Designed for theater exposure, they usually received treatment that was rough by any standard. Bends, tears, and rips are not uncommon flaws seen in lobby cards or posters.

A lobby card should be stored in an acid free plastic protector with an acid free board for solidity. You can also purchase transparent Mylar protectors for lobbies and avoid the backing boards. Lobbies can be stored upright, or stacked in acid free boxes and buffered properly. Direct light should be avoided; otherwise color bleaching may occur.

Posters are more difficult to store properly. Depending on the type of material — linen or thin gloss paper — the type of storage and protection can vary.

If the poster is paper, glossy or a flat finish, it should not be handled with bare hands. Oil from your hands can transfer to the poster, deteriorating the finish or leaving fingerprints on the surface. Warning: Even if you wear gloves, continual handling of a poster can lead to excessive wear on the fold area.

Because posters are so large, most people find flat storage impractical. Posters can be rolled, but it is not recommended unless the poster is protected by an acid free Mylar sheet.

Posters should be kept from high humidity, direct light, glass (lest the poster stick to the glass), smoke and heat.

Do not write on the back of posters, as bleeding can occur.

Do not apply tape to any poster unless the tape is archival quality and easily removed.

Like comic books, posters and lobby cards can be professionally restored. Restorers may offer such services as bleaching, spotting, relining, flattening, linen backing, and paper and color replacement.

Professional restoration is recommended if your items are valuable and showing serious signs of deterioration. The cost can vary, depending upon the services required. This marriage of chemistry and collecting is fascinating, and the results achieved can be quite miraculous!

Restoration is done by the following labs.

Linenback.com
Eugene Hughes
404 Lincoln Ave
Alexandria IN 45001
765-724-7613
www.linenback.com

Posterfix.com
Chris Clouotier
317 Washington Ave #2B
Brooklyn NY 11205
www.posterfix.com

Studio C
2129 Industrial Ct
Ste C
Vista CA 92083
800-583-8379
760-721-5528
www.atstudioc.com

Posterestoration.com
1101 S Robertson Blvd
Ste 201
Los Angeles CA 90035
310-276-3491
www.posterestoration.com

Poster Mountain
7320 Laurel Canyon Blvd
North Hollywood CA 91605
818-982-1058
www.postermountain.com

Recorded Media

There are many recording formats out there, all begging to be rescued from decay. Starting from Edison's wax cylinders to today's CDR/DVD technology, each medium presents challenges to those who wish to preserve it for future generations.

The formats that I shall discuss are reel to reel tape, album (78, 45, 33⅓), cassette tape, 8-track tape, film (nitrate, 8mm, 16mm), video tape (beta, VHS, digital), and DVD/CDR formats.

Consumer-recordable audio tape is a relatively recent phenomenon. Originally used as masters by the studios, reel to reel recording and playback units became available to consumers in the mid to late '60s. As a result, much archival material remains from that era. Professional recordings from the '50s onward are more rare (usually found in studio vaults), but still available. Reel to reel tape recorders were used professionally until the advent of digital recording. Digital Audio Tape (DAT) replaced reel to reel as the preferred format in the early '80s, and was in turn replaced in the late '90s by computer based hard drive storage or the CDR format.

Reel to reel type was the plaything of the audio buff. As a playback medium, tape didn't really go over big with consumers until 8-track players hit the market! From the early to the late '70s, 8-tracks were in. Compact discs entered the playback market in the early '80s. Later, mini disc, CDRs and the MP3 format contributed to the digital era.

In terms of consumer recording, reel to reel was replaced by the standard cassette. Until the popularity of digital recording increased, cassettes ruled the roost. DAT was preferred by the audiophile who did not have a reel to reel. These same people now use CDRs and the MP3 format to record their favorite music.

As for video recording, little was really available until Sony introduced the Beta format in 1975. For the first time, a consumer could record favorite shows at home. A revolution was born.

Until 1984, Beta was king, and when Sony and other manufacturers fought over copyright, JVC introduced us to the VHS format. With the introduction of personal video cameras from Sony and RCA, we were also able to record onto VHS, 8mm, Hi8, digital 8 and now mini digital video. Digital video recording hit the consumer in the mid '90s, and now we can record onto CDRs, or even onto DVDs with the appropriate software. The digital revolution is going on as we speak!

For video playback, we have had Beta, VHS, LD (laser disc), VD (video disk), S-VHS (better resolution), and DVD.

But, in the beginning of film, we had nitrate. That's where it all began — and where our memories have often faded and crumbled into video oblivion.

Nitrate film is volatile. Stored over a long period of time in an unventilated area, it can spontaneously burst into flame, or crumble to be lost forever! Stored in metal canisters in standard conditions, nitrate film can survive, and has survived for almost 100 years.

As varied as they are, video and audio tape formats all have similar needs when it comes to proper storage and preservation.

The environment should be cool (68 degrees), relatively dry (50 percent humidity), and most importantly, the tapes should be stored upright. Otherwise the tape on the reels can slip down and form a gentle arc. If this happens, the tapes may be damaged when played; they may tangle in the player because of the curl and improper tape movement across the heads, or the scratches from the downward pull from the tape reel will result in decreased video and audio quality.

One drawback of analog video or audio tape is signal dropout, for which there is no cure. Dropout is the loss of signal due to tape and data deterioration. Video dropout is easily detected as the colors or contrast will vary in intensity irregularly. Audio dropout occurs when the high and middle frequencies diminish in strength, resulting in muffled playback.

Color correctors can be used to reduce video dropout, and it is also possible to retape the show from a different source. With the ease of video editing on computers now, extensive dropout can be repaired, though the process is time consuming. Usually, the collector simply learns to live with flaw. Audio dropout cannot be repaired. Fortunately, with the DVD, CD, and computer formats, signal dropout should soon be a thing of the past.

If you do record on VHS, or analog cassettes, consider purchasing good-quality blank tapes, even if it means spending a little more. A higher quality tape will retain the signal for a longer time. As well, record video on the SP, or the shortest recording time. The better the detail on the recording, the longer the tape will retain good quality. As for audio tapes, normal bias tapes diminish in quality quickly. Chromium or metal tapes reproduce music and voice more faithfully due to their composition, and they retain signal over a longer time period.

Compact disc–based formats (CD, DVD, CDR) are easier to store. Because of their protective coating and casing, they can be stored upright or flat. They can be handled a little more roughly, and played more often without damage. More information can be stored on a CD than on 100 cassettes, so they are space efficient as well.

Nevertheless, these formats have some drawbacks. First, they scratch. If the scratch is deep enough, then that section of data is unplayable. (Small scratches can be repaired.) Second, the plastic coating used on the disc itself may not be stable over a long term, and stored data may be affected.

Often overlooked in discussions of magnetic media preservation is the importance of good equipment. A well maintained recording and playback unit (whether video or audio) can add years to your collection's life. Dirty heads, clogged heads, or bent guides on VCRs can easily destroy a perfect recording. This is especially true of the older formats. Beta machines and laser disc players cannot be purchased new, so maintenance of old players is vital to the preservation of older "archive" tapes and discs.

With the popularity of DVD players on the rise, VHS tapes will eventually become unavailable. And with that, VHS will join Beta, laser disc, reel to reel, and 8-tracks in the Recording Format Hall of Fame.

All of the advances in color and film technology have not proven to be the savior for the film industry, nor can digital techniques be depended on to preserve our treasures. At best, current technologies can be used to provide a backup of the originals, and to give today's moviegoers a glimpse of yesterday.

Metal Toys

Of all the collectibles we may have, metal toys are probably the most resistant to damage. Thanks to their sturdy construction, we do not usually have to strengthen any joints with acid free products, or coat them in plastic to keep them out of the air.

It is preferable, however, to keep the toys in their original packaging if possible. This will provide the best protection available for the toy, and all that remains is to provide an environment that makes the whole package crush-proof.

Rust is the greatest enemy to metal toys. The risk of rust can be lessened by careful repainting of the toy with a matching paint (if you want to), or by keeping the toy in an area of good ventilation and low relative humidity. If there is a rust patch, a light sanding can help to slow down the growth, and a basic solution applied to the immediate area may also help.

Metal toys can be stored (if not on your favorite shelf) in solid, acid free boxes in low humidity to keep excessive pH from the paint surface if it is unprotected.

Plastic Toys

Plastic toy preservation techniques are diverse. As materials evolve, preservation strategies change, meaning that older toys require different care than newer ones.

Generally speaking, all plastic toys should be kept out of direct sun.

Sunlight can cause the chemicals used to dye the plastic to deteriorate more quickly. Hard plastic toys will yellow with both age and exposure to UV radiation. If possible, a plastic toy should be kept in its original packaging in an environment free of structural stress. Toys can either be stored on shelving (for bragging purposes), or in solid, well protected boxes. When transporting toys, loose packing material should be stuffed around the toys to maintain their structural integrity.

Excessive moisture is generally not a concern to plastic toys, except that their paper packaging may decay. If you have the toy in its original packaging, the cardboard or paper may decay or mildew over time.

The pH of the storage environment may affect plastic toys. If the pH is too high or low, chemical reactions may occur on the plastic surface, causing damage. A pH neutral environment is suggested.

For toys with many parts, plastic storage bags may be used to keep the items together.

In terms of restoration, the choices are limited. Plastic toys can be washed in warm soapy water to clean oil and dirt from the surface, and cotton swabs (such as Q-Tips) dipped in bleach can be used to lighten stained areas. Where areas are broken, an experienced toy restoration expert can "plastic match'" to restore the integrity of the surface. Features such as strings, wheels, and moving parts such as gears can be repaired, and color chipping can be corrected.

Here are some contacts for toy restoration:

Randy's Toy Shop
165 North 9th St
Noblesville IN 46060
317-776-2220
www.randyshop.com

Tim-Oei Oei Enterprises, Ltd
241 Rowayton Ave
Rowayton CT 06853-1227
203-866-2470
(general toy restoration)

John Gibson
PO Box 40054
Washington DC 20016
301-527-0076
(Tootsie Toy restoration)

Cataloguing

Cataloguing is vital to the preservation of any collection. An accurate listing of your treasures is important for adequate insurance coverage, for the "I've got…" discussions with your buddies, and for preparing to sell or swap for something new.

Some things to consider listing when cataloguing your collectibles are character affiliation, item type, condition, production date if known, price paid, possible value, and identifying marks. It's a good idea to have a photograph of each item.

With the growing availability of user friendly computer programs, it is increasingly simple to create a database that will hold the above information, and sometimes even more. There are commercially available programs that track a comic book collection and actually update the retail value at the touch of a button. As of this writing, there is nothing similar for western collectibles.

For my video collection, I use Microsoft Works and list tape number, actor, title, year of production, start time, end time, tape speed, prerecord, value and genre.

Excel is useful because you can link to other databases with several "books" (spread sheet formats) accessible from any of the related listings. Excel is the most common tool used to customize databases for listings of all types.

Other useful cataloguing tools that can be used are file cards, sales catalogues (for posters and lobby cards), photographs, and price guides.

Of primary importance to cataloguing is photography. There have been several circumstances where items have been stolen from museums or collections but have been recovered thanks to photographs. Without photographs, it is difficult to properly identify collectibles in the absence of unique markings.

There is one distinct disadvantage to cataloguing your collectibles. If you have spent any time building a reasonable collection, when you sit down to catalogue it, time flies.

It is not a question of merely speeding through your favorite things in an evening or two. Every item you open, touch, or smell, you will remember. It may take five nights, six, a week. So, enjoy your time cataloguing. Slip a movie into the VCR or DVD, throw a disc into the CD player, boil up some coffee on the camp stove, and enjoy.

After you finish, you will have an objective list of your stuff. Catalogued as numbers and words, your collection is so many items, worth so much money, and occupies so much space.

This is collecting, reduced to its essential facts.

Insurance

Collectibles are hard to insure.

The biggest question that companies ask is, "How much is your collection worth?"

As a collector, you will probably answer with something like, "Well, somewhere around $... range."

"How much along the $... range?"

And so on.

Generally, the value of a collectible is difficult to peg down. Insurance companies will rarely pay what you feel your items are worth. Adding to the confusion is the absence of liquidity of collectibles, with the exception of CGC comic books and culturally recognized valuables. The difficulty is that collectibles are worth what someone wants to pay — no less, and no more.

Cataloguing is vital to your collectible insurance. The more information you have on your items, the more likely you are to recover stolen goods, or to receive a fair value in the event of a settlement.

A secondary consideration is appraisal. Expert appraisals are necessary to establish a baseline value that is acceptable to the insurance company and the appraiser. In this circumstance, the CGC grading is indispensable. Their word is final. You, as the collector, cannot establish a value for your own movie stills, books, or collectibles — at least not one that is authoritative financially speaking. An impartial expert must be called in. An expert may be the local collectibles dealer or an auction house. Sometimes even price guides can be used to establish inherent value.

Most companies do offer insurance on collectibles, but it is expensive unless the collectibles are considered under the household goods. Special conditions can be written into policies to increase limits on comics, books, artwork, or any other type of collectible that you may have. As a result, the majority of smaller collectors insure their "stuff" under their household goods. There is usually no difficulty as long as the total value of the claim is less than your household goods insurance value; if it is more, you may encounter difficulties. This is where the appraisal can help. Insurance is paid out on the basis of the insured value, which has been agreed to previously and is not disputed. It is vital, if you intend to insure your collectibles, to provide an accurate list for your insurer and to have an adequate limit set before any damage occurs.

Collectors with large inventories, should seek out special insurance. Shop around. The price may seem high, but if your collection is damaged beyond repair, you'll quickly understand the value of a good insurance policy.

Recently, collectible insurance has become more feasible with CGC standards in place. The Collectibles Insurance Agency provides a professional, impartial appraisal of your items. Highly recommended, they can be contacted at:

Collectibles Insurance Agency
PO Box 1200
Westminister MD 21158
1-888-837-9537
www.collectinsure.com

General Notes

The preservation of collectibles is largely common sense.

If we have a valuable book, don't use it as a paperweight.

If your *Gunsmoke* game is being crushed under a stack of comic books, move the game and strengthen the edges of the box. Store the comic books correctly.

If your Roy Rogers Nudie shirt is dirty and smells musty, clean it. If your folded movie posters are tearing at the folds, unfold them and mount them.

If an item is too far beyond a simple fix, talk to the experts. Take their advice. Your collectibles will thank you.

Although we are unable to control every factor that contributes to the gradual decay of our items, we should take as many steps as we can to preserve them. And we may have more control than we think. The science of paper preservation is growing. Thanks to ongoing research in Hollywood and beyond, the big screen classics of yesterday are being restored to their former glory, and forgotten films are finding new life. As more research takes place, the science of preservation is growing, and the techniques and technologies that result will help us all preserve the memory as well as the memorabilia. Collectibles that were once thought beyond repair may soon be almost pristine again.

9

Into the Sunset: The Future of Collecting

"Everybody off. Last stop until Kansas," the stagecoach driver says.

The passengers stir inside the coach, then slowly drift out of the double-wing doors. Massaging their backs and stretching tired, aching muscles, they enter the saloon.

The bartender, calmly wiping down a shot glass, smiles.

"Welcome to the Sunset Inn, folks, last stop before Purgatory. Best, and last, clean bath water for miles around. What can I get y'all?" He shoots a quick look at the tall man at the back. "Where'd ya get that Hopalong Cassidy lunch kit? I always wanted one. Care to trade for a clean bed and a bath?"

The tall man shakes his head. "I spent five years looking for this," he says. "Then my neighbor, who I've known for thirty years, up and gives it to me. Can you beat that? No, no matter how dirty or thirsty I am, no deal. However, if you have a copy of *Hoppy Takes a Writ*, I'll consider it."

The barkeep looks around.

"A steak, a shot of two-week-old whiskey, and a bath for a 1-sheet Tom Mix."

Nobody speaks.

"I've got a 2-sheet *Phantom Empire*, if that counts," a gangly passenger pipes up.

"Let's see."

The barkeep, holding the poster carefully, examines the edges, color bleeds, and roll.

"A steak and a bath. Shot of whiskey, half price."

The passenger looks nervous.

"Two shots of whiskey," he counters.

The two men take one step closer. They stare into each other's eyes and breathe deep. Reaching into his pocket, the barkeep pulls out a double eagle. Knowing what's coming, the other passengers step back.

"Heads you win. Tails, half price shot of whiskey," the barkeep says quietly.

"Flip."

The coin sails through the air, rotating madly in a high arc. Spinning faster, it lands on the floor. The barkeep kneels, then looks up and grins.

"Half price whiskey it is, stranger. Ante up!"

Another passenger digs into her bag and brings out a Tom Mix holster and gun set. Lovingly touching the pistol grips, she lifts them up.

"I'll trade, barkeep. I've only spent ten years looking for these. I really do need a warm bath and a comfortable bed. Is it a deal?"

The barkeep picks up the guns and looks down the barrels. Snapping the barrels back, he spins the cartridges. Nodding, he smiles.

"Baths for all of you. If I can rustle up some fresh meat, we'll have ourselves a party. Which of you has a copy of *Mexicali Rose*? Mine has a glitch in it. Leonard! Boil that water, we've got company!"

Well. This scene may never happen, but can you imagine it?

When we fans reach the end of our collecting years ... when, after lovingly sitting through thousands of hours of episodes, serials, and "Dusters," we have gathered the treasures of our youth around us ... what then?

The treasures of the past are safe.

With two new museums being built to commemorate the silver screen cowboys (Roy Rogers in Branson and Hopalong Cassidy in Kansas), and the recent opening of the National Cowgirl Museum in Fort Worth, the remastering and restoration of the Republic properties, the restoration of the Hopalong Cassidy movies and episodes, and the revivals of classic characters like the Lone Ranger, the future of the culture is assured.

As the children and grandchildren of the stars, and those who have inherited the mantles of the icons, look to new venues for presentations of classic, character forming-entertainment, we can look toward the light and see more than a sliver of hope. It seems that many people are reaching out for familiar things with nostalgic appeal. Record-breaking auctions have been held recently for comic books, locks of Elvis' hair, hardcovers, and even the estates of famous stars. Prices for rare and authentic items are skyrocketing. At the same time, the reproduction industry is flourishing. Knock-offs of rare items frequently turn up and sell for top dollar, while originals sell for pennies on the dollar during online bidding.

There is an increased demand, and thirst for shows with integrity. Independent western productions, and even a few big-budget features, are still being made. There is no William Witney, Whitey Hughes, nor a Joe Kane to backstop lavish, toe tapping, all-out-western action films with singing cowboys and delicate cowgirls—but the 2003 release of the splashy *Open Range*, with Kevin Costner and Robert Duvall, gave lovers of western movies plenty to get excited about.

Annie Get Your Gun is a recent western-flavored success on Broadway. *Lonesome Dove*, based on the Larry McMurtry novel, was a successful mini-series and television show. *Dr Quinn, Medicine Woman* successfully ran for many seasons, propelling Jane Seymour and Joe Lara into the annals of television history. The Lone Ranger, Gene Autry, Zorro, Hopalong Cassidy, *Gunsmoke*, *Bonanza*, and Roy Rogers all make regular appearances on the specialty networks.

Are westerns dead?

They are not dead; they are different. We, the fans who once thrilled to the adventures of our favorite cowboys (or cowgirls) on radio, TV and the big screen, are also different. Our tastes have changed, as we have. But we still long for heroes. Who doesn't? And as long as there are heroes, there will be westerns.

Is the sunset approaching?

Ask the 50,000 fans who swarmed the Santa Clarita Cowboy Poetry Festival. Ask the fans who attend the many film festivals around North America. Ask the artists. Ask the surviving movie and television stars who are continually surprised by the attention they receive. If you could ask them, what would Roy Rogers, Gene Autry, Dale Evans, and Clayton Moore think of their loyal fans?

Is the sunset approaching?

Not even close.

After attending a local antique show, I was struck by the mid–50s crowd milling about, mulling over the items, pausing to touch and admire the comics, books, figurines, posters, clothes, and games featuring the heroes of their youth. Excited youngsters listened while grandparents explained who the Lone Ranger, Roy Rogers, and Zorro were. Middle-aged children picked up rare comic books, and whispered to each other, and smiled.

Did they remember the heroes?

Without a doubt. To their dying breath, they will remember their heroes from the silver screen and the lessons they were taught.

"To have a friend, you must first be one."
"Respect your parents."
"Be polite to ladies."
"Don't take chances." (Sure Roy, sure.)

As the fans and collectors spoke, a familiar refrain echoed through the air.

"Whoa. Giddy up, boy. Let's go, Trigger."
"Hi Yo Silver, away!"
"Let's go, Champ."
"Ah, Nellybelle!"

The trail is waiting...

Bibliography

Drew, Bernard A. *Hopalong Cassidy: The Clarence E. Mulford Story.* Scarecrow, 1991.

Felbinger, Lee. *The Lone Ranger Pictorial Scrapbook.* Countryside Publishing, 1988.

Hake, Ted, ed. *The Official Hake's Price Guide to Character Toys,* 4th ed.

Hancer, Kevin. *Hancer's Price Guide to Paperback Books,* 3rd ed. Wallace-Homestead Book Company, 1990.

Holland, Dave. *From Out of the Past: A Pictorial History of the Lone Ranger.* Holland House, 1988.

Hudgeons, Thomas E., ed. *The Official Price Guide To Radio-TV & Move Memorabilia.* House of Collectibles, 1986.

Hutchison, Don. *The Great Pulp Heroes.* Mosaic Press, 1998.

Liljeblad, Cynthia Boris. *TV Toys and the Shows That Inspired Them.* Krause Publications, 1996.

Overstreet, Robert M. *The Official Overstreet Comic Book Price* Guide. Avon Books, 2002.

_____. *Official Overstreet Comic Book Price Guide Companion.* House of Collectibles, 1991.

Stephan, Elizabeth, and Dan Stearns, eds. *O'Brien's Collecting Toys: Identification and Value Guide.* Krause Publications, 1999.

Web Sites

Without the tremendous resources available on the Internet, this book would not be a reality. My reference sources include:

www.amazon.com
www.eBay.com
www.abe.com
www.royrogers.com
www.breyerhorses.com

And many, many others too numerous to mention. Thanks to all.

Index